Decorating
Your Home with
Cross-Stitch

Decorating Your Home with Cross-Stitch

Donna Kooler

A Sterling/Chapelle Book

Sterling Publishing Co., Inc. New York

For Chapelle Limited

Owner: Jo Packham

Staff: Trice Boerens, Rebecca Christensen, Holly Fuller, Cherie Hanson, Holly Hollingsworth, Susan Jorgensen, Lorin May, Tammy Perkins, Jamie C. Pierce, Leslie Ridenour, Amy Vineyard, Nancy Whitely, and Lorrie Young

Photographers: Ryne Hazen
Kevin Dilley

The photographs in this book were taken at the homes of Jo Packham and Edie Stockstill and at R C Willey in Salt Lake City, UT.

Items in this book were graciously provided by the following: Adam Original of Cottage Grove, NC; Alpha Omega Woodcraft of Morro Bay, CA; Chapelle Designers of Ogden, UT; Charles Craft of Laurinburg, NC; Darice Incorporated of Strongsville, OH; DMC of South Kearney, NJ; Leisure Arts of Little Rock, AR; Peking Handicrafts of South San Francisco, CA; Sudberry House of Old Lyme, CT; Wichelt Imports of Stoddar, WI; and Zweigart of Somerset, NJ.

Library of Congress Cataloging-in-Publication Data

Kooler, Donna.
    Decorating your home with cross-stitch / by Donna Kooler.
       p. cm.
    "A Sterling/Chapelle book."
    Includes index.
    ISBN 0-8069-0988-9
    1. Cross-stitch—Patterns. 2. Household linens. 3. Textile fabrics in interior decoration. I. Kooler Design Studio. II. Title.
TT778.C64K663 1995   95-30300
746.44'3—dc20   CIP

10 9 8 7 6 5 4 3 2 1

A Sterling/Chapelle Book

Published by Sterling Publishing Company, Inc.
387 Park Avenue South, New York, N.Y. 10016
© 1995 by Chapelle Ltd.
Distributed in Canada by Sterling Publishing
℅ Canadian Manda Group, One Atlantic Avenue, Suite 105
Toronto, Ontario, Canada M6K 3E7
Distributed in Great Britain and Europe by Cassell PLC
Villiers House, 41/47 Strand, London WC2N 5JE, England
Distributed in Australia by Capricorn Link (Australia) Pty Ltd.
P.O. Box 6651, Baulkham Hills, Business Center, NSW 2153, Australia
Printed and bound in Hong Kong
All Rights Reserved

Sterling ISBN 0-8069-0988-9

For Kooler Design Studio, Inc.

President: Donna Kooler

Vice President: Linda Gillum

Senior Designer: Nancy Rossi

Staff Designers: Barbara Baatz, Holly DeFount, Jorja Hernandez, and Sandy Orton

Creative Director: Deanna Hall West

Project Coordinator: Priscilla Heden

Design Assistants: Sara Angle, Anita Forfang, Virginia Hanley–Rivett, Marsha Hinkson, Arlis Johnson, Lori Patton, Char Randolph, Gina Tarricone, and Pam Whyte

Contributing Project Constructionist: Laurie Grant

Framer: Frame City, Pleasant Hill, CA 94533

<u>**Decorating Your Home**</u>
<u>**with Cross-Stitch**</u>
<u>**Rooms and Designers**</u>
Front Door – Barbara Baatz
Living Room – Barbara Baatz
Toddler's Room – Linda Gillum
Kitchen – Linda Gillum
Dining Room – Sandy Orton
Bathroom – Holly DeFount
Master Bedroom – Jorja Hernandez
Family Room – Nancy Rossi

For information on where to purchase specialty items in this book, please write to:

Customer Service Department
Chapelle Designers
204 25th Street, Suite 300
Ogden, UT 84401

*To my mother, Rose Sherman Harris,
who gave me the appreciation for
fine needlework.*

Donna Harris Kooler

 Donna Kooler founded the Kooler Design Studio, which has become world famous for its outstanding needlework designs. The studio holds claim to having gathered together the most creative, versatile and well-known needlework designers in America. Their diverse backgrounds and training have proved to be an award-winning combination. Each designer brings her own perspective to a project, adding a distinct flavor to the mix. As in any recipe, you need many ingredients to make the final creation successful.

Welcome
to a
Cross-Stitcher's Dream Home

All of us at the Kooler Design Studio lovingly decorate our own homes with needlework accents and we wanted to share our designs and home decor projects with you. The rooms in our dream house were designed separately by several artists from the studio. Although each of us brings our uniqueness and natural style to this book, these cross-stitch designs produce harmony and unity in each room.

The designs and projects throughout this book are timeless and versatile. They could easily highlight any room, regardless of decorating style — traditional, country, victorian or even "early matrimonial." Although we've used the Pansy-n-Ivy theme in the master bedroom, the same designs would be wonderful in a bright sun room filled with white wicker furniture, or the dining room's Carnation Sampler and clock would make an entry hall a warm and welcoming area.

It's these cross-stitch touches that make rooms unique and truly personal — definitely a home for all seasons.

CONTENTS

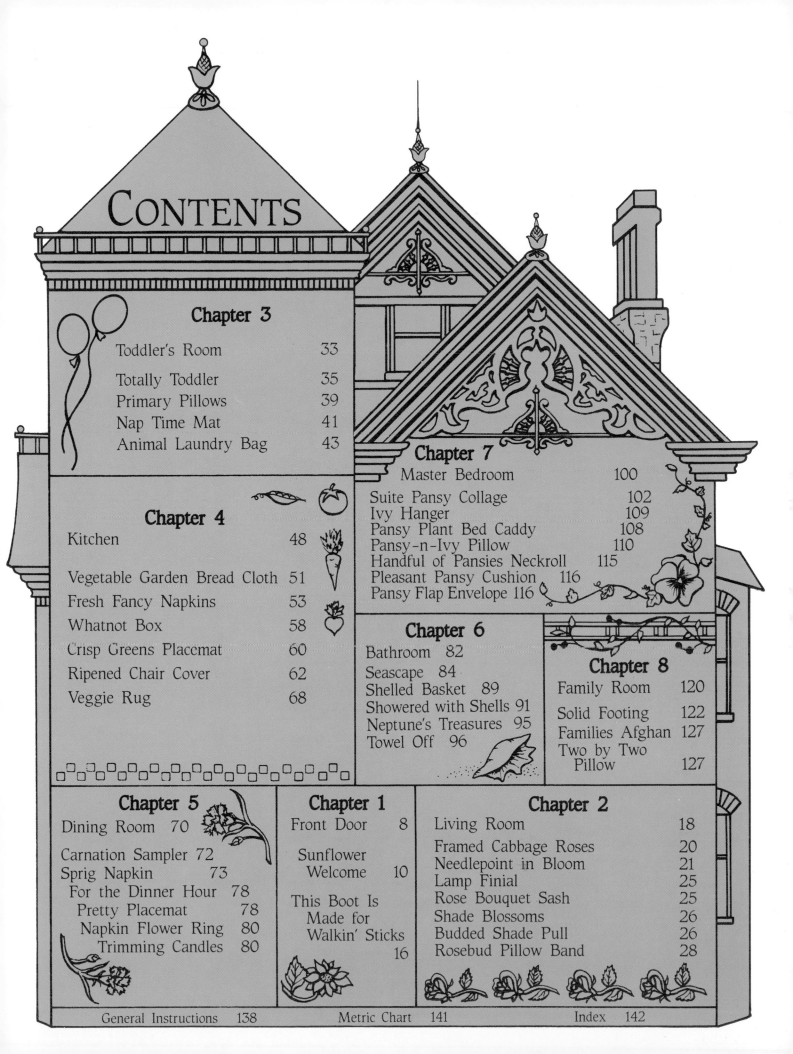

FRONT DOOR

*A house is built of logs and stone,
Of tiles and posts and piers;
A home is built of loving deeds,
That stand a thousand years.*

Victor Hugo

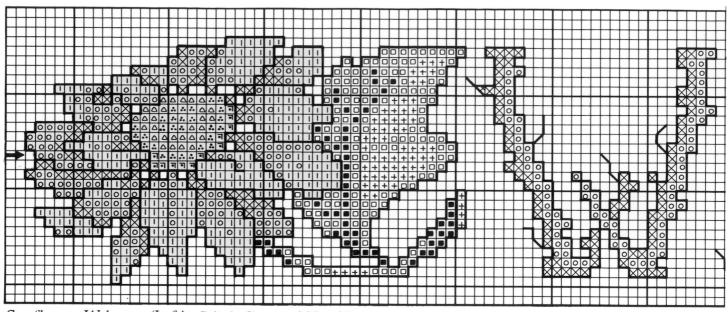

Sunflower Welcome (Left)　**Stitch Count: 222 x 27**

TheSunflower Welcome band is stitched on white-on-white linen 28 banding over two threads, the finished design size is 15⅞" x 1⅞". The fabric was cut 23" x 3". The Sunflower Wreath design is stitched on a pre-made ivory 10 muslin-ruffled pillow cover over one thread, the finished design size is 9⅝" x 9⅜".

Sunflower Welcome Band

FABRIC	DESIGN SIZES
Aida 11	20⅛" x 2½"
Aida 14	15⅞" x 1⅞"
Aida 18	12⅜" x 1½"
Hardanger 22	10⅛" x 1¼"

Sunflower Wreath Design

FABRIC	DESIGN SIZES
Aida 11	8¾" x 8½"
Aida 14	6⅞" x 6¾"
Aida 18	5⅜" x 5¼"
Hardanger 22	4⅜" x 4¼"

MATERIALS

Completed Sunflower Welcome design
Completed Sunflower Wreath design
½ yard of black-and-tan checkered fabric
14" of ⅝"-wide black grosgrain ribbon
¾ yard of ⅜"-diameter cotton cord
Sewing thread: white and black
10½"-square cardboard or foam core
⅜ yard of thick quilt batting
18" x 3½" x ½" piece of pine board
¼ yard of medium-weight fusible interfacing
Flat black acrylic spray paint
Paint sealer and disposable foam brush
#220 sandpaper
Two ⅝" cup hooks
Two 1"-wide sawtooth hangers
Hand stapler and staples

DIRECTIONS

1. Make cording using cotton cord and 2½"-wide bias-cut strip of checkered fabric (2" longer than perimeter of pillow cover at ruffled seam).

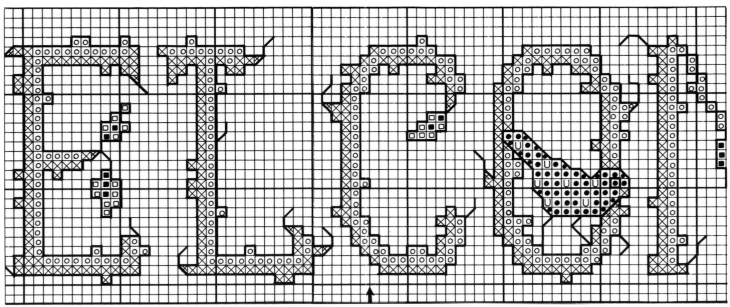

Sunflower Welcome (Middle)

2. Hand-sew cording to pillow cover, beginning and ending cording at base of pillow. Turn under fabric on one end and slip other end into it, making a clean join.

3. Cut wider ribbon into 7" lengths and press under each cut end ¼". Tack one folded end to pillow cover front 1½" from side seam, hiding tack under cording. Tack other end of ribbon to pillow cover back 1½" from side seam. Repeat for other ribbon.

4. To make "pillow form," trim quilt batting to width of foam core. Wrap batting around foam core one-and-one-half times and trim. Overcast cut edges of batting, enclosing foam core. Insert this padded form into pillow cover with the thicker padded side adjacent to the design back. Zip pillow closed and set aside.

5. Cut fusible interfacing same dimensions as banding fabric. Following manufacturer's instructions, adhere interfacing to back of Sunflower Welcome design fabric.

6. Sand and seal pine board.

7. Spray-paint board, let dry, and sand smooth. Repeat this procedure as many times as necessary. Do not sand after last coat of paint.

8. Screw cup hooks into base of board 5" from ends.

9. Center and wrap design fabric around board. Staple design ends to back of board.

10. Attach sawtooth hangers 3" from each end of board.

11. Cut narrow ribbon in half; tie bow with each half and tack to cup hooks. Decoratively trim ribbon ends.

12. Hang pillow on Sunflower Welcome design.

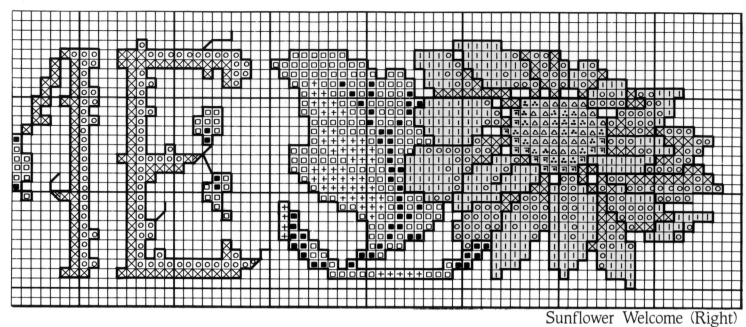

Sunflower Welcome (Right)

Sunflower Wreath (Top Left)   **Stitch Count: 96 x 94**

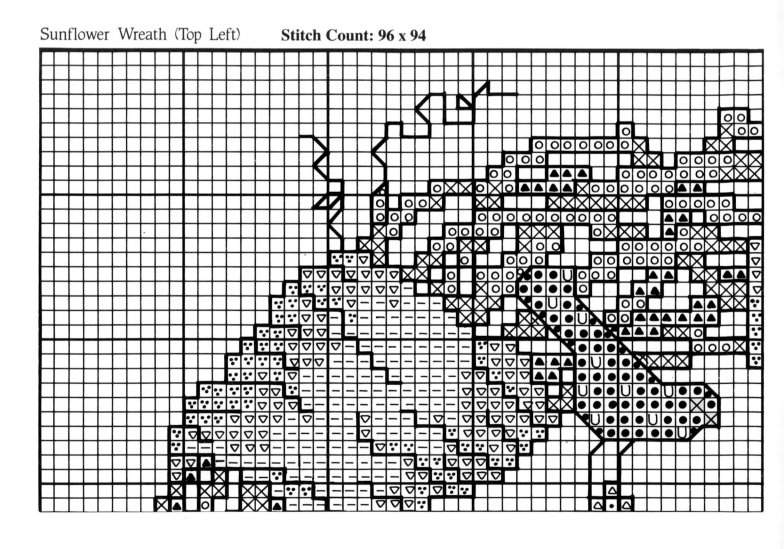

Anchor   DMC (used for sample)

Step 1: Cross-stitch (3 strands for Welcome Band)
(4 strands for Pillow)

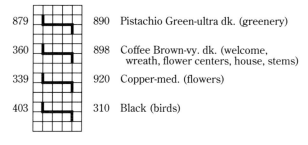

Anchor			DMC	Color
1	U	╱		White
926	·	╱		Ecru
301	I		744	Yellow-pale
303	O		742	Tangerine-lt.
304	X		741	Tangerine-med.
214	+		368	Pistachio Green-lt.
243	□		988	Forest Green-med.
246	■		986	Forest Green-vy. dk.
886	−		3047	Yellow Beige-lt.
887	▽		3046	Yellow Beige-med.
373	∴		3045	Yellow Beige-dk.
944	╱		869	Hazel Nut Brown-vy. dk.
362	○	◸	437	Tan-lt.
309	X	╱	435	Brown-vy. lt.
371	▲	◿	433	Brown-med.
360	◙		898	Coffee Brown-vy. dk.

Anchor			DMC	Color
349	△	◿	921	Copper
351	∴		400	Mahogany-dk.
400	╱	╱	414	Steel Gray-dk.
403	●	◿	310	Black

Step 2: Backstitch (1 strand for Welcome Band)
(2 strands for Pillow)

Anchor		DMC	Color
879		890	Pistachio Green-ultra dk. (greenery)
360		898	Coffee Brown-vy. dk. (welcome, wreath, flower centers, house, stems)
339		920	Copper-med. (flowers)
403		310	Black (birds)

Sunflower Wreath (Top Right)

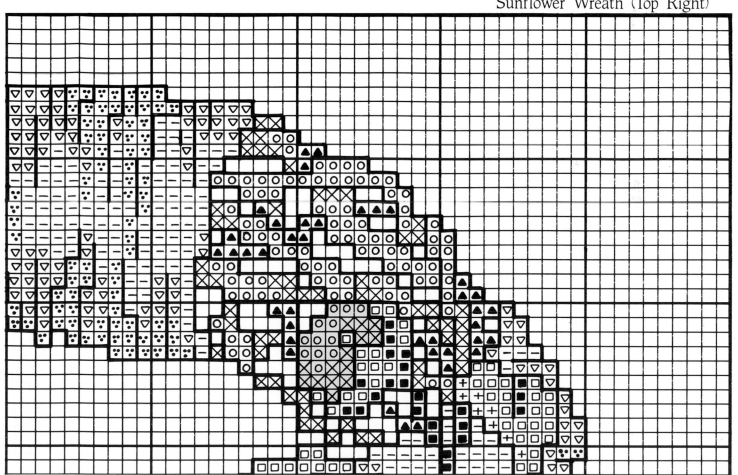

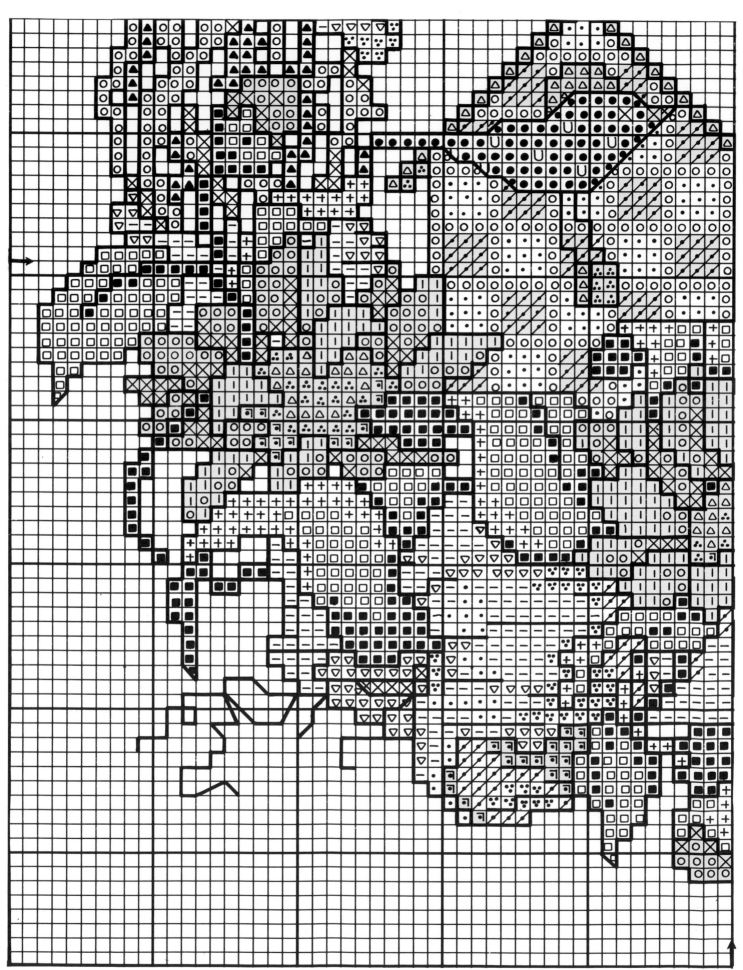

Sunflower Wreath (Bottom Left)

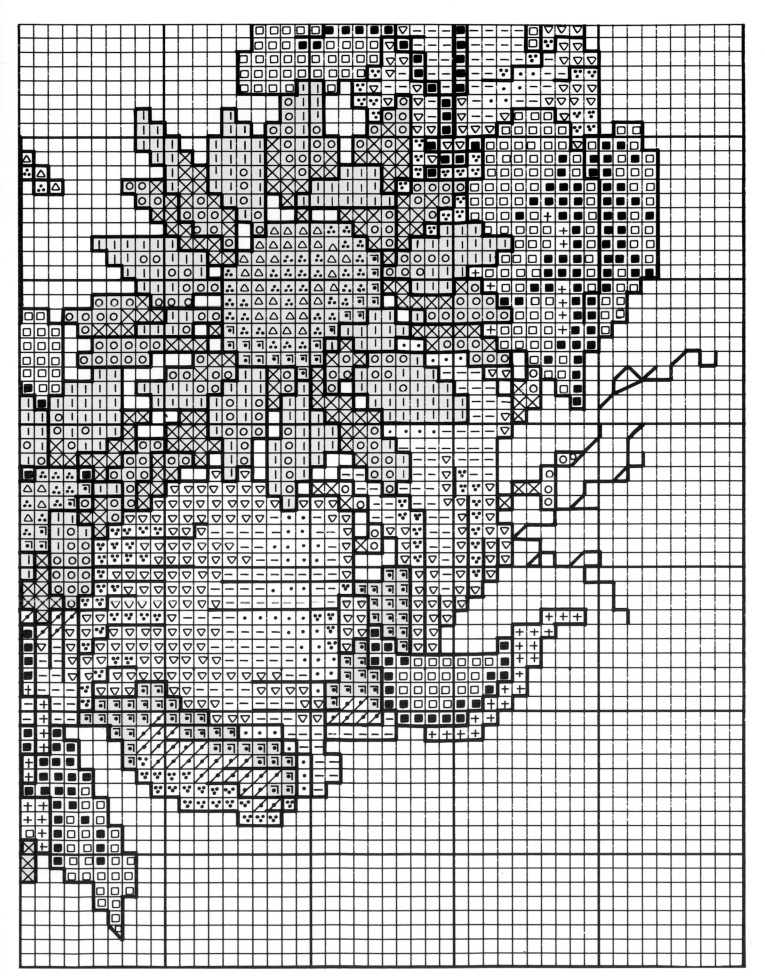

Sunflower Wreath (Bottom Right)

MATERIALS

Plastic stocking form (14" high)
1 yard of black-and-tan checkered fabric
½ yard of muslin (boot lining)
Ecru sewing thread
Sand or smooth gravel
Silk sunflowers, wooden bird, twigs, raffia, natural-
    colored twisted paper for floral arrangement
Hot glue gun and glue sticks

DIRECTIONS

All seam allowances are ½".

1. Enlarge patterns on photocopy machine 150 per-cent . From both muslin and black-and-tan checkered fabric, cut two stockings and one sole each.

2. With right sides facing, stitch muslin stockings together along center front seam. Press seam open. Turn top long edge ¼" to wrong side; stitch. With rights sides facing, stitch center back seam. Turn. Repeat for black-and-tan checkered stocking.

3. Fold muslin sole piece in half lengthwise to find center; mark. With right sides facing, pin sole to bottom edge of muslin stocking, matching center with seams. Beginning with heel, stitch pieces together with right sides facing and raw edges aligned. Turn. Repeat for black-and-tan checkered stocking.

4. Slide black-and-tan checkered stocking onto plastic boot. With wrong side out, stuff muslin stocking inside plastic boot. Fold top edge of muslin stocking over 1". Matching top edges of both stockings, tack the two stockings together.

5. Measure 9½" down from center top, make a box pleat, and tack. Center and decoratively arrange sunflowers, birds, twigs, raffia and twisted paper bow at pleat. Hot-glue in place.

6. Fill stocking one-fourth to one-third full with sand or gravel to hold umbrella and walking sticks.

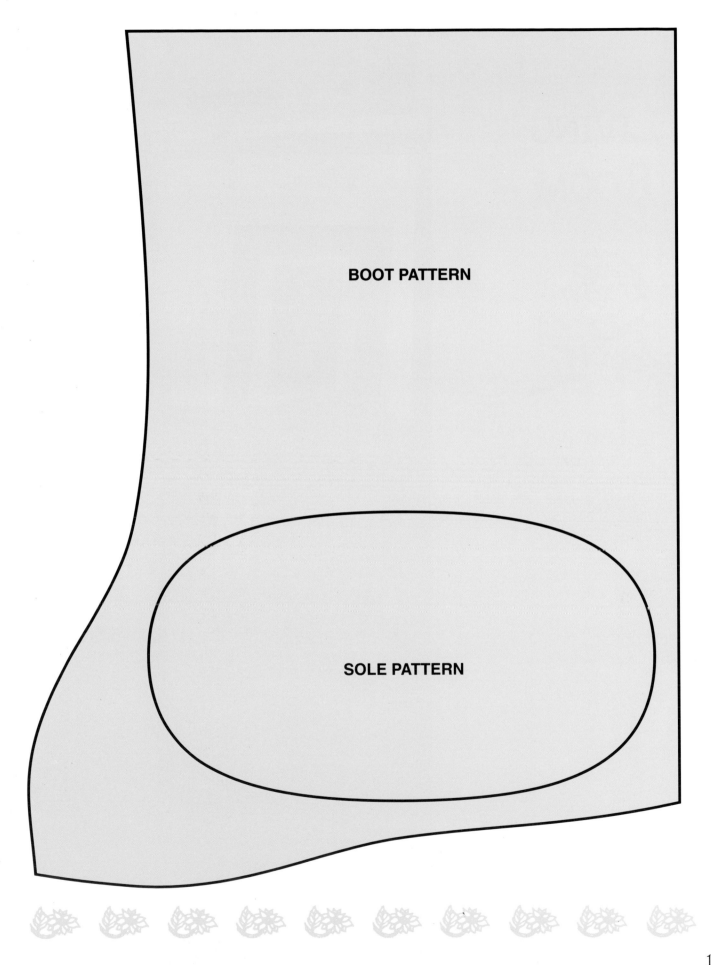

BOOT PATTERN

SOLE PATTERN

LIVING ROOM

One should always put a little magic into their home. By the fireplace, put a glass bottle filled with nine needles, nine pins, and nine nails. It keeps out the bad fairies, you know!

FRAMED CABBAGE ROSES

Stitched on cream Pastel Linen 28, over two threads, the finished design size is 11¼" x 9⅞". The fabric was cut 25" x 24". See photo on page 19.

FABRICS	DESIGN SIZES
Aida 11	14⅜" x 12⅝"
Aida 14	11¼" x 9⅞"
Aida 18	10½" x 9¼"
Hardanger 22	7⅛" x 6⅜"

Paternayan Persian Yarn **DMC (used for framed sample)**

Step 1: Cross-stitch (3 strands)

260	+		White
947	·	818	Baby Pink
945			776	Pink-med.
944	△	899	Rose-med.
942	✕	309	Rose-deep
969	○	321	Christmas Red
900	●	815	Garnet-med.
907	·	3689	Mauve-lt.

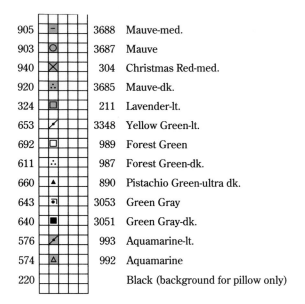

905	⊟	3688	Mauve-med.
903	○	3687	Mauve
940	✕	304	Christmas Red-med.
920	∴	3685	Mauve-dk.
324	⊡	211	Lavender-lt.
653	╱	3348	Yellow Green-lt.
692	▢	989	Forest Green
611	∴	987	Forest Green-dk.
660	▲	890	Pistachio Green-ultra dk.
643	⊓	3053	Green Gray
640	■	3051	Green Gray-dk.
576	╱	993	Aquamarine-lt.
574	△	992	Aquamarine
220			Black (background for pillow only)

Step 2: Backstitch (for framed sample only: 1 strand)

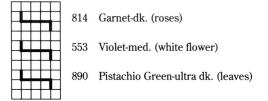

	814	Garnet-dk. (roses)
	553	Violet-med. (white flower)
	890	Pistachio Green-ultra dk. (leaves)

Framed Cabbage Roses (Top Left)   **Stitch Count: 158 x 139**

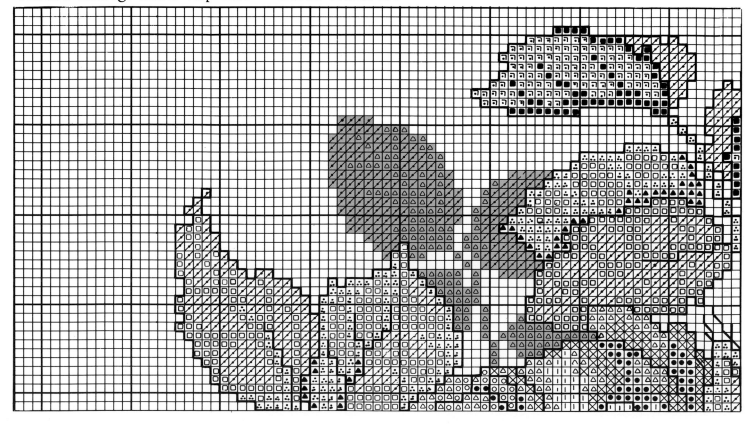

NEEDLEPOINT IN BLOOM

Stitched on mono canvas 10 over one thread, the finished design size is 11¼" x 9⅞". The stitch count is 158 x 139. The fabric was cut 20" x 22". See photo on page 24.

MATERIALS

Completed design on mono canvas 10
Persian-type wool yarn (see code for colors)
½ yard black damask upholstery-weight fabric; matching thread
2 yards of ⅜"-wide black twisted cord with lip (available at upholstery shops)
Black cord-and-tassel tieback unit (5½"-long tassel)
Stuffing

DIRECTIONS

All seams are ½".

1. Block needlepoint.

2. Baste and sew cording around edges of stitching, overlapping ends at bottom edge and rounding corners slightly.

3. Trim canvas even with tape on cording.

4. Using design fabric as pattern, cut backing from black fabric.

5. With right sides facing, baste and sew design fabrics and backing fabric together, leaving a 6" opening along bottom edge. Clip corners and turn right side out.

6. Stuff pillow firmly. Slipstitch opening closed.

7. Tack loops of tieback unit to pillow front along top seam line, 2" from right side and with equal-length loops on either side of tack.

8. Tack bead of tieback unit 1" below seam line to form a loose bow.

Framed Cabbage Roses (Top Right)

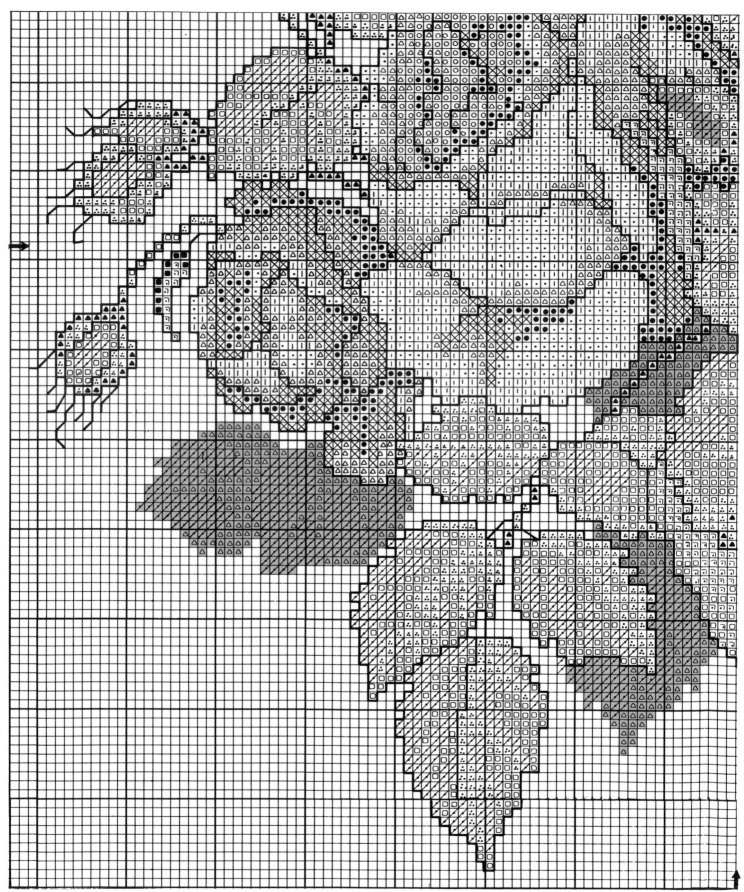

Framed Cabbage Roses (Bottom Left)

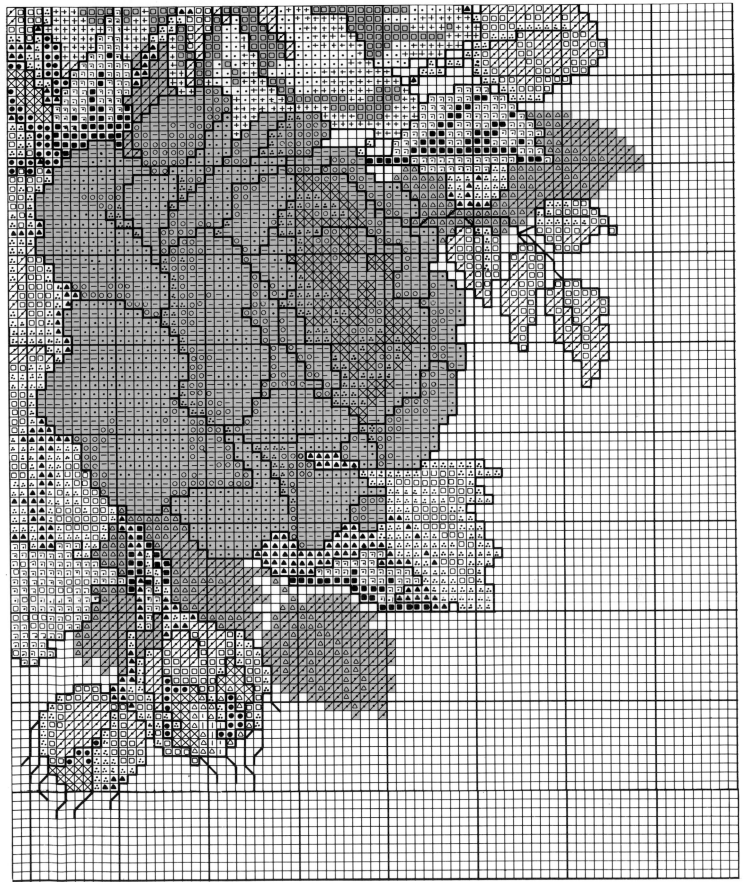

Framed Cabbage Roses (Bottom Right)

Lamp Finial

The design for the Rose Blossom is taken from the graph on page 30. Use the code on page 20. Stitched on perforated plastic 14 over one thread, the finished design size is 2⅝" x 2½". The plastic was cut 4" x 4". See photo page 29.

FABRIC	DESIGN SIZES
Aida 11	3¼" x 3⅛"
Aida 14	2⅝" x 2½"
Aida 18	2" x 2"
Hardanger 22	1⅝" x 1⅝"

MATERIALS
Completed design
1 ½" flat round lamp finial (available at lamp stores)
3"-square medium-weight cardboard
3"-square burgundy cotton damask fabric
Invisible sewing thread
Thick fabric glue

DIRECTIONS
1. Cut perforated plastic one square away from stitched design.

2. Trace around design on the cardboard and cut ⅛" in from the tracing line. Check to be sure that the cardboard extends only as far as the stitching and not beyond to the perforated plastic. Continue to trim cardboard as necessary.

3. For the backing, lightly glue fabric to side of cardboard that is not adjacent to back of stitching. Trim fabric to within ¼" of cardboard, pull fabric edges to back of cardboard; glue, clipping where necessary.

4. Hand-sew design piece and backing piece together, using the invisible thread. Leave a 1½" opening at base of design piece.

5. Insert metal lamp finial.

Rose Bouquet Sash

The design for the Cabbage Rose Border is taken from the graph on page 30. Use the code on page 31. Stitched on white-on-white linen banding 28 over two threads, the finished design size is 9¾" x 2". The fabric was cut 28" x 2¾". For tieback for left-side curtain, begin stitching left side of design 2¼" from left side of banding and centered top and bottom. For tieback for right-side curtain, begin stitching left side of design 12⅝" from left side of banding and centered top and bottom. See photo page 29.

FABRIC	DESIGN SIZES
Aida 11	12½" x 2½"
Aida 14	9¾" x 2"
Aida 18	7⅝" x 1½"
Hardanger 22	6¼" x 1¼"

MATERIALS
Completed design
Four 23" x 2⅝" pieces of heavy-weight iron-on interfacing
Two white corded tiebacks with tassels
22" of ⅛" white twisted cord
White sewing thread
Thick fabric glue

DIRECTIONS
All seam allowances are ½".

1. Following manufacturer's instructions, center and apply two layers of interfacing (one at a time) to the back of each design.

2. Zigzag ends of banding. Pleat and tack ends so that width of banding is 1¼" wide

3. Cut twisted cord length into 5½" lengths. Apply glue to ends to prevent raveling. After glue has dried, overlap cord ends ½" and tack together. Fold one end of banding under ½", enclosing corded loop, and tack in place. Repeat for all banding ends.

4. Tie a looped bow with corded tieback and tack to front of tieback ¾" from corded loops.

SHADE BLOSSOMS

The design for Cabbage Rose Border and Rosebud are taken from the graphs on page 30 and code on page 31. Stitched on white-on-white linen banding 28 over two threads, the finished design size is 24¾" x 2". The fabric was cut 2" longer than width of window shade x 2¾". Begin stitching by centering Cabbage Rose Border design and follow with Rosebuds on right and left side. If shade is wider than 18", then stitch additional Rosebud designs spaced 2" from the main border design and from each other. Add as many Rosebud designs as necessary for a pleasing appearance. The photographed shade is 36" wide.

Cabbage Rose Border

FABRIC	DESIGN SIZES
Aida 11	12½" x 2½"
Aida 14	9¾" x 2"
Aida 18	7⅝" x 1½"
Hardanger 22	6¼" x 1¼"

Rosebud

FABRIC	DESIGN SIZES
Aida 11	2¼" x 2⅛"
Aida 14	1¾" x 1⅝"
Aida 18	1⅜" x 1¼"
Hardanger 22	1⅛" x 1"

MATERIALS
Completed design
Fabric window shade (width determined by window size)
Medium-weight iron-on interfacing (width and length of linen banding)
White sewing thread
Fabric glue
1"-wide sponge brush

DIRECTIONS
1. Center banding over shade and trim ends ½" beyond shade width.

2. Trim interfacing 2⅝" wide and 1" shorter than band. Following manufacturer's instructions, center and apply interfacing to back of design fabric.

3. Zigzag ends of banding.

4. Dilute glue with water until glue is of a spreadable consistency but not watery. Apply a thin layer of glue to the back of the design peice. Center banding right side up over shade and 1¼" from bottom of shade, making sure banding is straight and not wrinkled. Let dry.

5. Turn shade over and glue banding ends to back of shade.

6. Attach shade pull.

BUDDED SHADE PULL

The design for the Rosebud is taken from the graph on page 30 and use the code on page 31. Stitched on perforated plastic 14 over one thread, the finished design size is 1¾" x 1⅝". The fabric was cut 3" x 3".

FABRIC	DESIGN SIZES
Aida 11	2¼" x 2⅛"
Aida 14	1¾" x 1⅝"
Aida 18	1⅜" x 1¼"
Hardanger 22	1⅛" x 1"

MATERIALS
Completed design
White window shade string pull unit
3"-high white tassel
3"-square piece of burgundy cotton damask fabric
3"-square piece of medium-weight cardboard
Invisible sewing thread
Thick fabric glue

DIRECTIONS
1. Cut perforated plastic one square away from stitched design.

2. Trace around design on the cardboard and cut ⅛" in from the tracing line. Check to be sure that the cardboard extends only as far as the stitching and not beyond to the perforated plastic. Continue to trim cardboard as necessary.

3. For the backing piece, lightly glue fabric to side of cardboard that is not adjacent to back of stitching. Trim fabric to within ¼" of cardboard, pull fabric edges to back of cardboard; glue, clipping where necessary. Set aside.

4. Cut ring from string pull piece. Trim string cord to 6". Fold in half and glue ½" of raw cord ends to back of design at center top.

5. Glue tassel hanger to back of design at center bottom.

6. Glue backing piece to design piece, wrong sides together. Hand-sew design piece and backing piece together, using the invisible thread. Tack several times where cord and backing piece meet.

7. Loop design piece cord behind decorative shade screw and attach to window shade.

ROSEBUD PILLOW BAND

The design for the Cabbage Rose Border is taken from the graphs on pages 30 and use the code on page 31. Stitched on white-on-white linen banding 28 over two threads, the finished design size is 9¾" x 2". The fabric was cut 28" x 2¾".

FABRIC	DESIGN SIZES
Aida 11	12½" x 2½"
Aida 14	9¾" x 2"
Aida 18	7⅝" x 1½"
Hardanger 22	6¼" x 1¼"

MATERIALS
Completed design
25" x 2⅝" piece of heavy-weight iron-on interfacing
½ yard of burgundy damask cotton fabric; matching thread
Stuffing

DIRECTIONS
All seams are 1/2".

1. Cut burgundy fabric into two 18½" squares.

2. With right sides facing, sew burgundy fabric together, leaving a 6" opening on one side.

3. Clip corners and turn right side out.

4. Stuff pillow firmly and slipstitch opening closed.

5. Hand-sew a running stitch line across middle of pillow front, gather to desired effect, and secure thread. Set aside.

6. With design piece centered, trim fabric to 26".

7. Following manufacturer's instructions, apply interfacing to back of design fabric.

8. Zigzag each end of design fabric, press under ⅜", and stitch.

9. Wrap design fabric around middle of pillow (squeezing pillow into an hourglass shape), overlap ends ⅜", and slipstitch closed.

The question is not, he notes, whether you can come home again, but whether you ever really leave...

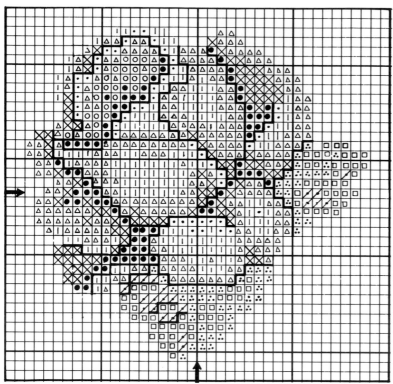

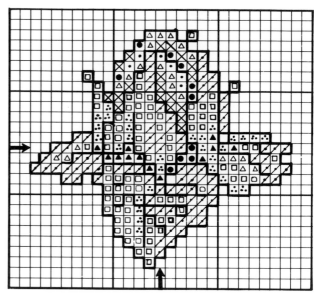

Rosebud **Stitch count: 25 x 23**

Rose Blossom **Stitch count: 36 x 35**

Cabbage Rose Border **Stitch count: 137 x 28**

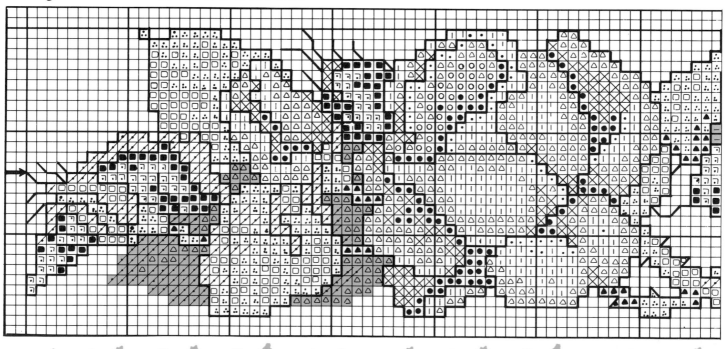

Anchor   **DMC (used for sample)**

Step 1: Cross-stitch (3 strands)

48	·	818	Baby Pink
24	I	776	Pink-med.
27	△	899	Rose-med.
42	✕	309	Rose-deep
43	●	815	Garnet-med.
46	∪	321	Christmas Red
49	▪	3689	Mauve-lt.
66	−	3688	Mauve-med.
69	○	3687	Mauve
70	U	3685	Mauve-dk.
47	✕	304	Christmas Red-med.
44	∴	814	Garnet-dk.
265	╱ ╱	3348	Yellow Green-lt.
242	▢ ◿	989	Forest Green
244	∴ ◿	987	Forest Green-dk.

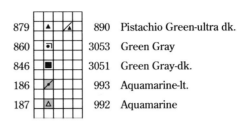

879	▲ ◿	890	Pistachio Green-ultra dk.
860	◙	3053	Green Gray
846	■	3051	Green Gray-dk.
186	◪	993	Aquamarine-lt.
187	△	992	Aquamarine

Step 2: Backstitch (1 strand)

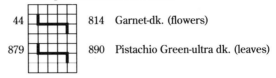

44		814	Garnet-dk. (flowers)
879		890	Pistachio Green-ultra dk. (leaves)

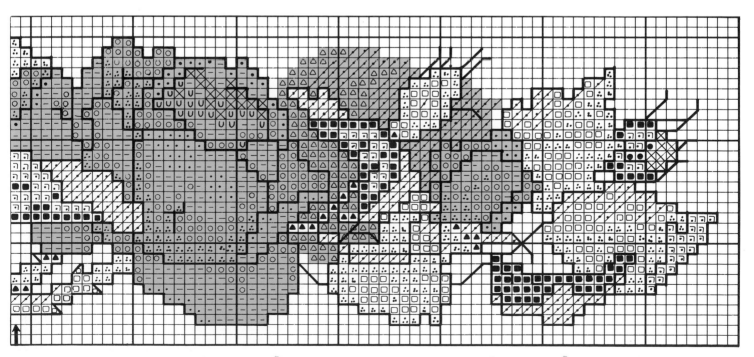

TODDLER'S ROOM

*She could hear them living all
through the house.*

Great-grandma Spaulding

TOTALLY TODDLER

Stitched on white Aida 14 over one thread, the finished design size is 14⅞" x 7⅞". The fabric was cut 21" x 14".

FABRICS

FABRICS	DESIGN SIZES
Aida 11	18⅞" x10"
Aida 18	11½" x 6⅛"
Hardanger 22	9½" x 5"

Anchor			DMC (used for sample)	
Step 1: Cross-stitch (3 strands)				
1	·			White
881	−		945	Peach Beige
297	+		743	Yellow-med.
298	▽		972	Canary-deep
50	⊡		605	Cranberry-vy. lt.
335	△		606	Orange Red-bright
47	✕		321	Christmas Red
130	◇		799	Delft-med.
131	∴		798	Delft-dk.
132	○		797	Royal Blue
86	▨		3608	Plum-vy. lt.
204	I		912	Emerald Green-lt.
347	△		402	Mahogany-vy. lt.
349	▲		921	Copper
378	□		841	Beige Brown-lt.
380	■		839	Beige Brown-dk.
398	╱		415	Pearl Gray
400	∴		414	Steel Gray-dk.
403	●		310	Black

Step 2: Backstitch (1 strand)

380		839	Beige Brown-dk. (yellow balloon, head and body on raccoon, tiger and bear, face of tiger, stuffed bear, bear on book)
403		310	Black (face on raccoon and panda, eyes on tiger, hippo and bear, black areas of panda)
401		413	Pewter Gray-dk. (all else)

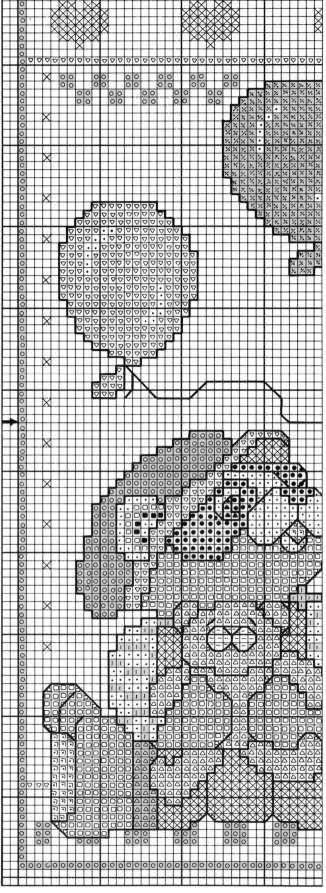

Stitch Count: 209 x 110

35

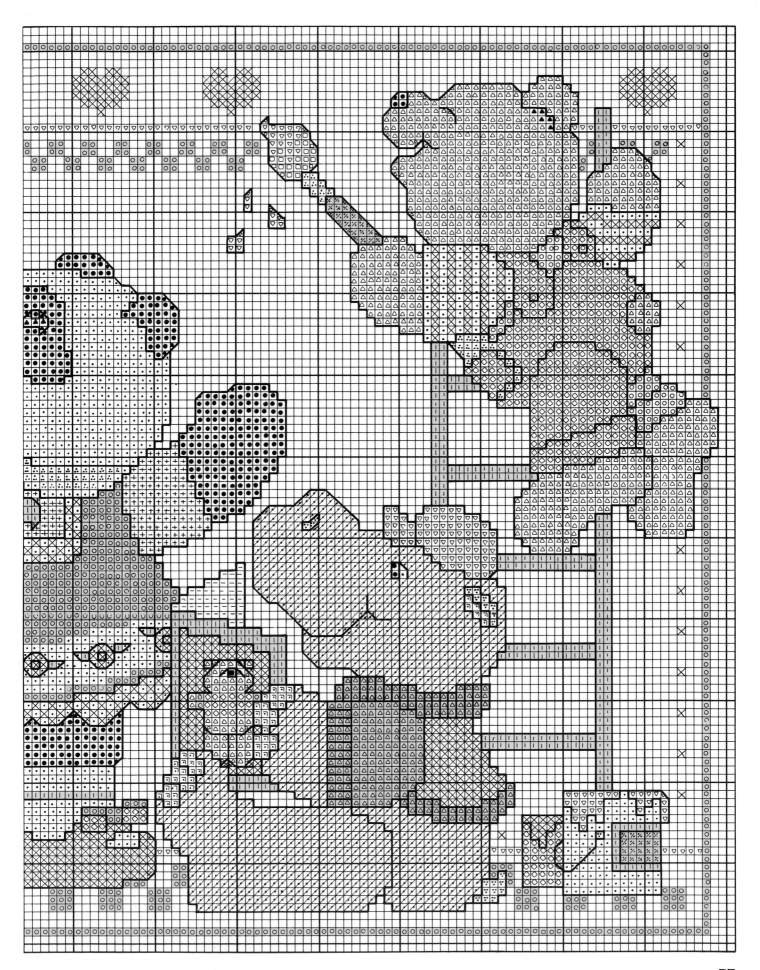

PRIMARY PILLOWS

Stitched on white Herta 6 over one thread, the finished design size is 6⅞" x 6⅛" for the Panda and 5⅞" x 5⅜" for the Racoon. The fabric was cut 15" x 15" for each. The designs were taken from the graph and code on page 35.

Panda Pillow

FABRICS	DESIGN SIZES
Aida 11	3¾" x 3⅜"
Aida 14	2⅞" x 2⅝"
Aida 18	2¼" x 2"
Hardanger 22	1⅞" x 1⅝"

Stitch Count: 41 x 37

Racoon Pillow

FABRICS	DESIGN SIZES
Aida 11	3⅛" x 3"
Aida 14	2½" x 2¼"
Aida 18	2" x 1¾"
Hardanger 22	1⅝" x 1½"

Stitch Count: 35 x 32

MATERIALS
Completed design (Raccoon or Panda)
¾ yard of multi-striped polished cotton fabric
⅜ yard of fleece
1 yard of ⅜" red piping
2 yards of size 5 white or ecru perle cotton
Stuffing
Cream sewing thread
Straight pins

DIRECTIONS
All seam allowances are a ½".

1. Trim design fabric to 9½" square. For Raccoon design, place fish 1" from left side seam with rest of design centered from top and bottom; for Panda design, place balloon 1" from right side seam with remaining design centered from top and bottom.

2. Cut one 9½" square from striped fabric for pillow backing. Cut one 9½" square from fleece. Baste fleece to back of design fabric.

3. Cut and piece striped fabric into a 69" x 7" strip to make the ruffle. With right sides facing, sew short sides of strip together, making a loop. Press the seam open.

4. Fold ruffle in half lengthwise, wrong sides facing, and press. With a medium-distanced zigzag stitch, stitch over the perle cotton ¼" from the raw edge. Fold the ruffle into quarters and mark with pins. Using the perle cotton, run a gathering stitch along zigzagged edge of ruffle; pull thread, gathering ruffle to fit design fabric.

5. Baste piping around front of design fabric, matching raw edges and beginning and ending at base of design. Turn under one end of piping and slip other end into it, making a clean join.

6. Matching raw edges and aligning pins with corners of design fabric, baste ruffle around front of fabric, sandwiching piping. Allow more gathers at corners to prevent ruffle from cupping inward.

7. With right sides facing, sew striped backing to design unit, leaving a 5" opening at the bottom. Trim the corners and turn.

8. Firmly stuff pillow. Slipstitch opening closed.

Nap Time Mat

Stitched on a pre-made quilted nap mat with an 8 ½"-wide white Monk's Cloth 6 insert over one thread, the finished design size is 32" x 7⅛". Center and stitch design, omitting checkerboard line and name. Center and stitch name, from Block alphabet on page 46, between yellow lines. Cross-stitch checkerboard motif, stopping adjacent to name.

FABRICS
Aida 11
Aida 14
Aida 18
Hardanger 22

DESIGN SIZES
17½" x 4¼"
13¾" x 3⅜"
10¾" x 2⅝"
8¾" x 2⅛"

Anchor			DMC (used for sample)	
Step 1: Cross-stitch (6 strands)				
1	·		White	
881	▣		945	Peach Beige
297	+		743	Yellow-med.
298	▽		972	Canary-deep
304	■		741	Tangerine-med.
335	◇		606	Orange Red-bright
50	%		605	Cranberry-vy. lt.
47	□		321	Christmas Red
86	△		3608	Plum-vy. lt.
130	−		799	Delft-med.
131	✕		798	Delft-dk.
132	○		797	Royal Blue
206	·		955	Nile Green-lt.
204	□		912	Emerald Green-lt.
347	△		402	Mahogany-vy. lt.
349	▲		921	Copper
378	╱		841	Beige Brown-lt.
380	●		839	Beige Brown-dk.
398	○		415	Pearl Gray
403	∴		310	Black

Step 2: Backstitch (2 strands)

204	912	Emerald Green-lt. (fishing line, stripes in racoon's shirt, bear picture)
349	921	Copper (fish)

380	839	Beige Brown-dk. (racoon body, bear bodies, bird's beak)
401	413	Pewter Gray-dk. (fishing reel, balloon, hippo's body, racoon's hat and shirt, book, bear's shirt, crayon, picture, panda's dress and head)
47	321	Christmas Red (4 strands - book, bear's shirt, heart, picture hooks, balloon string)
403	310	Black (all else)

Step 3: French Knot (4 strands)

403	●	310	Black

Nap Time Mat (Left)

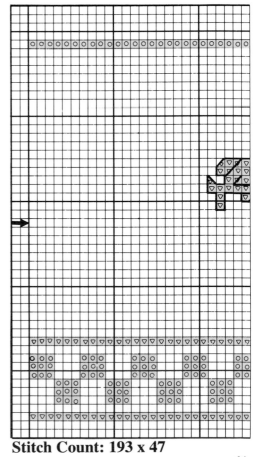

Stitch Count: 193 x 47

 41

Nap Time Mat (Middle)

Nap Time Mat (Right)

Stitched on a pre-made laundry bag with a 3½"-wide blue Aida 14 insert over one thread, the finished design size is 14¾" x 3⅛". Center and stitch design omitting the name. Using the Crayon Alphabet on page 46, center and stitch name in the space between the bear and the hippo. If the name is longer than nine letters, choose a shorter version or nickname. Allow two spaces between each letter.

FABRICS

FABRICS	DESIGN SIZES
Aida 11	18⅞" x 4"
Aida 18	11½" x 2⅜"
Hardanger 22	9⅜" x 2"

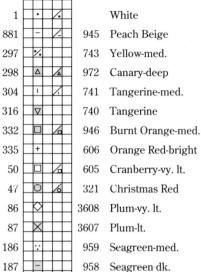

Anchor			DMC (used for sample)
		Step 1: Cross-stitch (3 strands)	
1	·	∕	White
881	−	∕	945 Peach Beige
297	⁒		743 Yellow-med.
298	▲	∕	972 Canary-deep
304	ı	∕	741 Tangerine-med.
316	▽		740 Tangerine
332	□	◿	946 Burnt Orange-med.
335	+		606 Orange Red-bright
50	□	◿	605 Cranberry-vy. lt.
47	○	◿	321 Christmas Red
86	◇		3608 Plum-vy. lt.
87	✕		3607 Plum-lt.
186	∷		959 Seagreen-med.
187	−		958 Seagreen-dk.

Animal Laundry Bag (Left) **Stitch Count: 207 x 43**

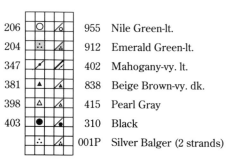

206	○	◿	955	Nile Green-lt.
204	∴	◿	912	Emerald Green-lt.
347	╱	╱	402	Mahogany-vy. lt.
381	▲	◿	838	Beige Brown-vy. dk.
398	△	◿	415	Pearl Gray
403	●	◿	310	Black
	∴	◿	001P	Silver Balger (2 strands)

Step 2: Backstitch (1 strand)

47		321	Christmas Red (wheels on skates, laces)
381		838	Beige Brown-vy. dk. (bear's face and hands)
403		310	Black (all else)

Step 3: French Knot (1 strand)

| 403 | ● | 310 | Black |

Animal Laundry Bag (Middle)

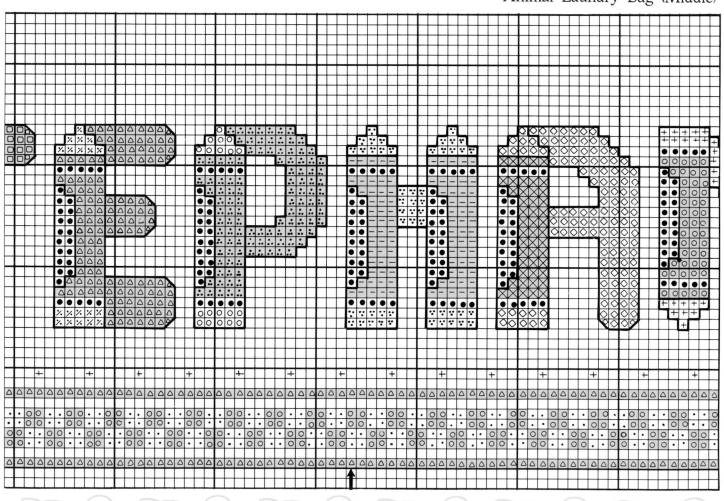

Animal Laundry Bag (Right)

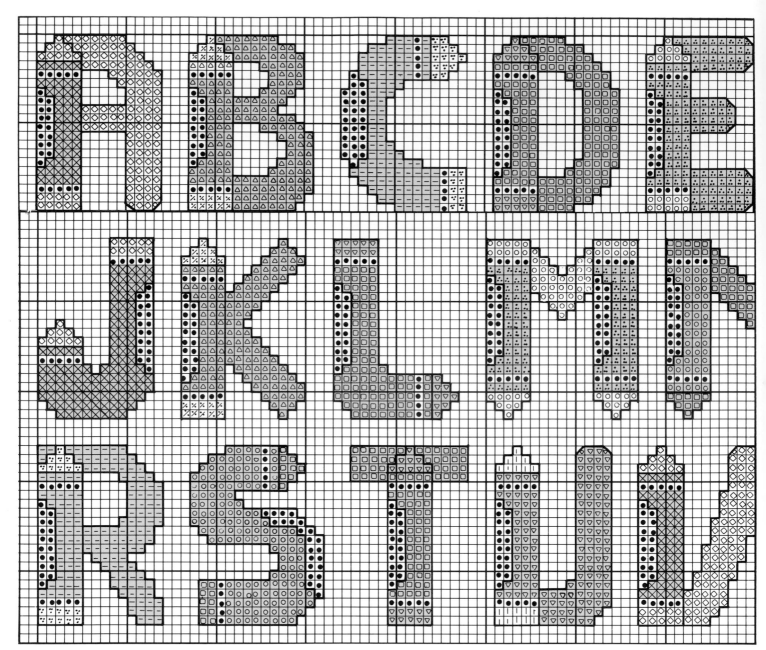

Crayon Alphabet

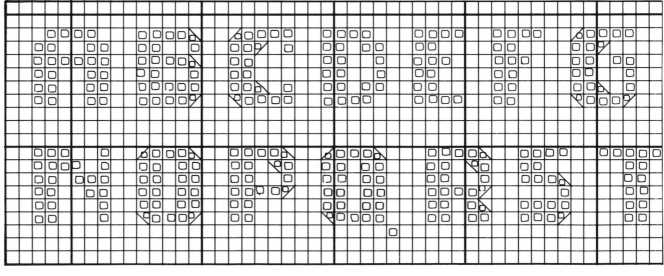

Block Alphabet

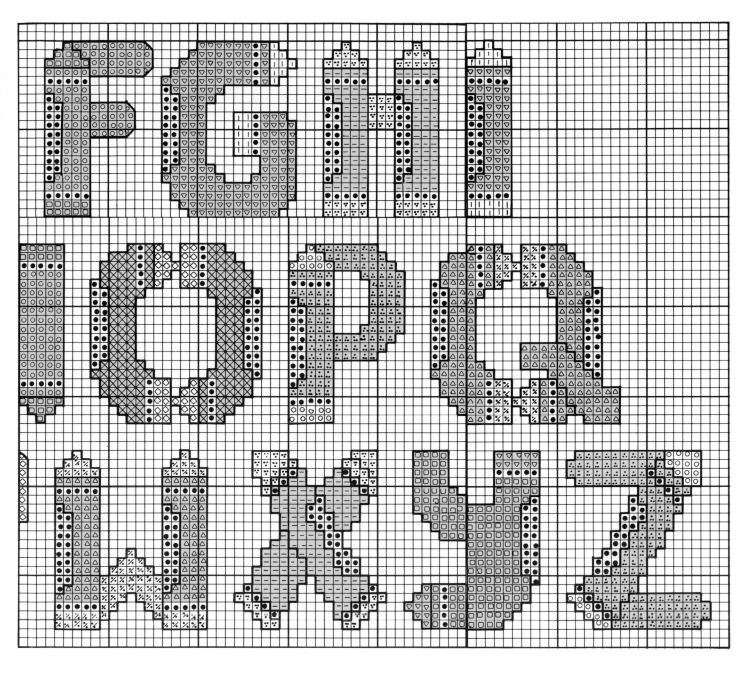

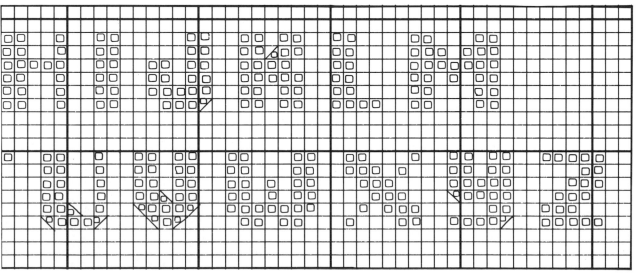

KITCHEN

The best conversations happen around our kitchen table. Many times we have laughed, cried, shared feelings, hopes and dreams; sorted out differences; solved the problems of the world; recognized our strengths and weaknesses into the wee hours of the morning.

VEGETABLE GARDEN BREAD CLOTH

Stitched on ivory Aida 14 over 1 thread, the finished design size is one-fourth of the complete design at 7¾" x 7¾". The fabric for the complete cloth was cut 20" x 20". Begin stitching with the garnet box 2" from the corner edges. Repeat for all corners and continue the garnet line to connect the corner designs.

FABRIC
Aida 11
Aida 18
Hardanger 22

DESIGN SIZES
9⅞" x 9⅞"
6" x 6"
5" x 5"

MATERIALS
Completed design
⅛ yard black fabric
Black sewing thread

DIRECTIONS

1. Trim the design fabric to 1" beyond the garnet boxes (bread cloth should be 18" square).

2. Cut and piece the black fabric into a 76" x 1⅝" strip. Fold it in half lengthwise and press.

3. Pin the binding strip to the front of the design fabric and align raw edges, mitering corners if desired; where the binding strip ends meet, fold one end back ½" and overlap the other end (trim away excess fabric). Sew the binding strip and design fabric together ¼" from the raw edges. Fold the binding to the back of the design fabric and hand-stitch together. Take care that the stitches do not show on the front (again mitering corners if desired).

Anchor   **DMC (used for sample)**

Step 1: Cross-stitch (3 strands)

Anchor		DMC	
323	– ⁄	722	Orange Spice-lt.
43	∴	815	Garnet-med.
76	⊙ ⊿	961	Wild Rose-dk.
264	ı	772	Pine Green-lt.
209	✕	913	Nile Green-med.
228	■	910	Emerald Green-dk.
942	•	738	Tan-vy. lt.
403	⊙	310	Black

Step 2: Backstitch (1 strand)

228		910	Emerald Green-dk. (inside veins of lettuce)
403		310	Black (all else)

Vegetable Garden Bread Cloth
Stitch Count: 109 x 110

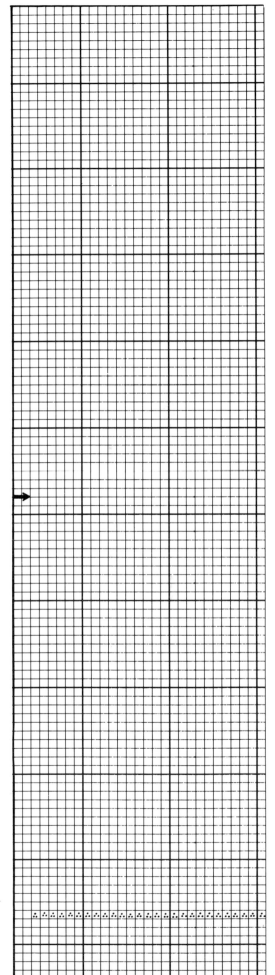

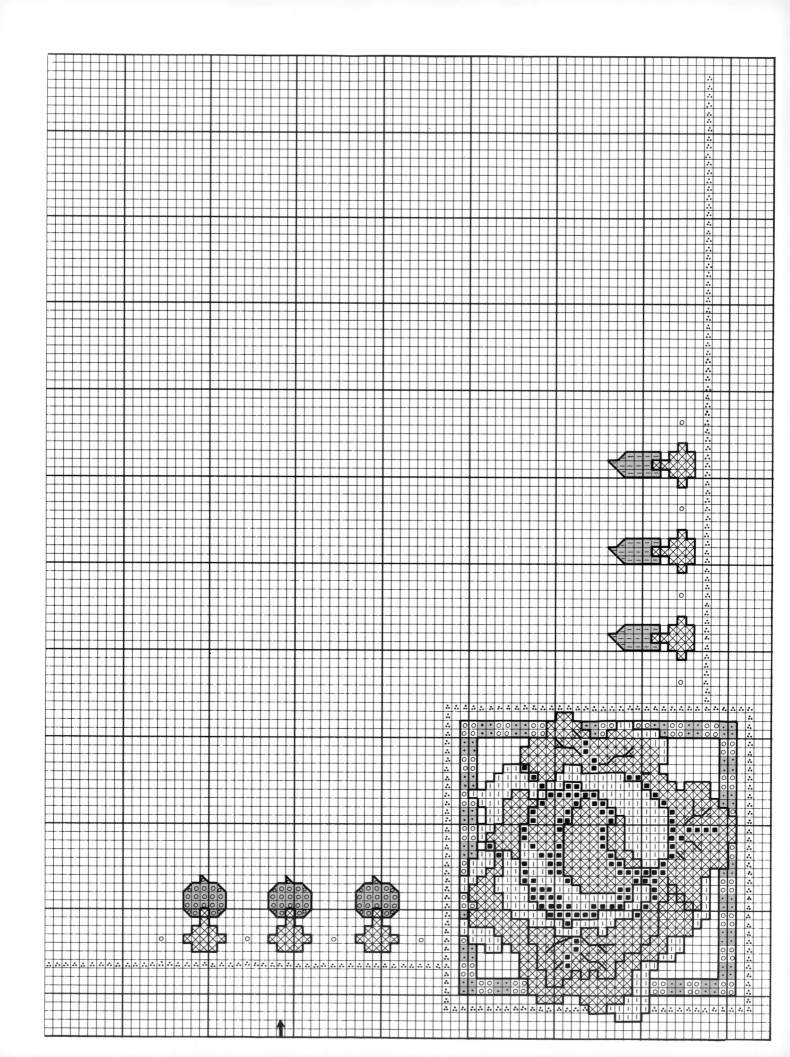

FRESH FANCY NAPKINS

Stitched on ivory Aida 14 over 1 thread, the finished design size is 3⅞" x 4" for the peas, 3⅞" x 3⅞" for the carrots, 4⅛" x 4¼" for the tomatoes, and 4⅛" x 4⅛" for the radishes. The fabric for each design was cut 18" x18". Begin stitching each design with the garnet box 2" from one corner.

Peas

FABRIC	DESIGN SIZES
Aida 11	4⅞" x 5⅛"
Aida 18	3" x 3⅛"
Hardanger 22	2½" x 2½"

Carrots

FABRIC	DESIGN SIZES
Aida 11	4⅞" x 4⅞"
Aida 18	3" x 3"
Hardanger 22	2½" x 2½"

Tomatoes

FABRIC	DESIGN SIZES
Aida 11	5⅛" x 5½"
Aida 18	3⅛" x 3⅜"
Hardanger	2⅝" x 2¾"

Radishes

FABRIC	DESIGN SIZES
Aida 11	5¼" x 5¼"
Aida 18	3¼" x 3¼"
Hardanger 22	2⅝" x 2⅝"

MATERIALS (for one napkin)
Completed designs
⅛ yard of black fabric; matching thread

DIRECTIONS
1. For each napkin, trim the design fabric to 15" square with the garnet box ⅞" from the corner edges.

2. Cut and piece the black fabric into a 65" x 1⅝" strip. Fold it in half lengthwise and press.

3. Pin the binding strip to the front of the design fabric and align raw edges mitering corners if desired; where the binding strip ends meet, fold one end back ½" and overlap the other end (trim away excess fabric). Sew the binding strip and design fabric together ¼" from the raw edges. Fold the binding to the back of the design fabric and hand-stitch together. Take care that the stitches don't show on the front (again mitering corners if desired).

Anchor		DMC (used for sample)	
	Step 1: Cross-stitch (3 strands)		
1			White
323		722	Orange Spice-lt.
324		721	Orange Spice-med.
335		606	Orange Red-bright
47		321	Christmas Red
43		815	Garnet-med.
76		961	Wild Rose-dk.
42		3350	Dusty Rose-dk.
264		772	Pine Green-lt.
209		913	Nile Green-med.
228		910	Emerald Green-dk.
942		738	Tan-vy. lt.
403		310	Black

	Step 2: Backstitch (1 strand)		
43		815	Garnet-med. (inside carrots)
228		910	Emerald Green-dk. (tomatoe stems)
403		310	Black (all else)

Tomatoes   **Stitch Count: 57 x 60**

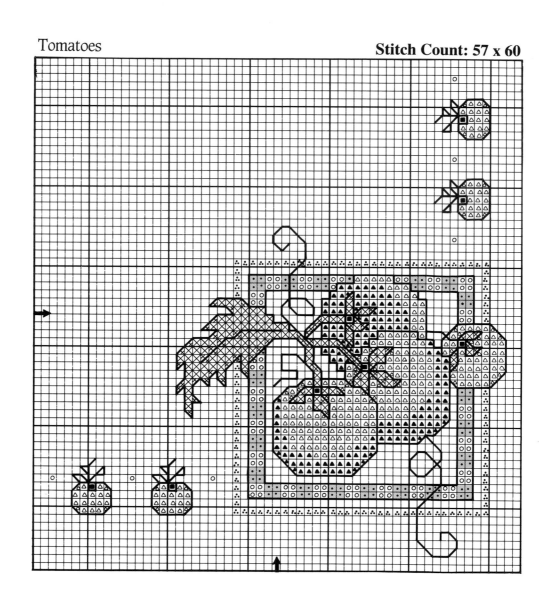

54

Carrots

Stitch Count: 54 x 54

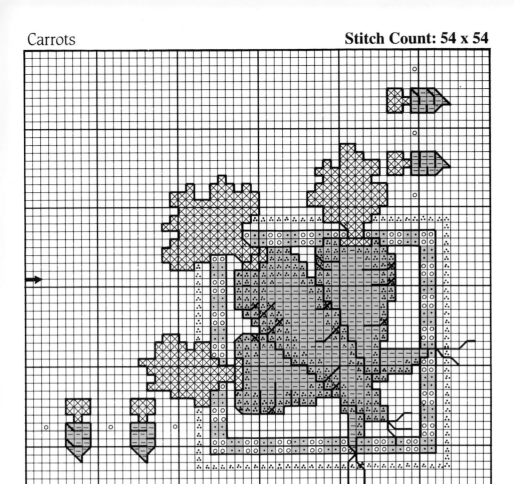

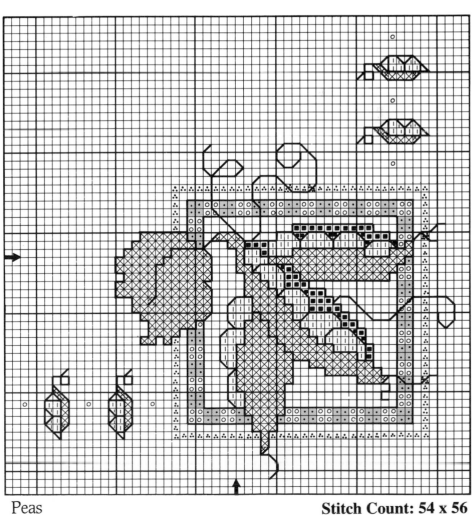

Peas

Stitch Count: 54 x 56

Stitch Count: 58 x 58

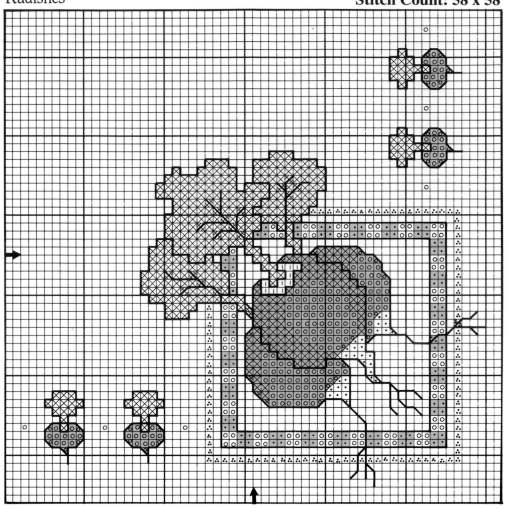

WHATNOT BOX

Stitched on ivory Aida 14 over one thread, the finished design size is 3¾" x 3¾". The fabric was cut 8" by 8".

FABRIC   **DESIGN SIZES**
Aida 11   4¾" x 4¾"
Aida 18   2⅞" x 2⅞"
Hardanger   2⅜" x 2⅜"

MATERIALS
Completed design
6"-square piece of coordinating fabric
5¼" x 4½" wooden desk box
Two 4⅜"-square pieces of lightweight cardboard
4⅜"-square piece of fleece
Thick fabric glue
Glazier points

DIRECTIONS
1. Trim design fabric to 5½"-square with design centered.

2. Glue fleece to one peice of cardboard.

3. Center design fabric, right side up, on top of fleece. Pull fabric edges to back of cardboard and glue.

4. For backing board, center remaining fabric over second piece of lightweight cardboard, pull fabric edges to back of cardboard, and glue.

5. Insert design piece into box and secure with glazier points.

6. Glue backing piece to design piece, wrong sides together.

7. Option: To use as a doorstop or bookend, make a small sandbag from muslin (5" x 7" folded and sewn) and fill with sand (about half a pound); insert into box for weight.

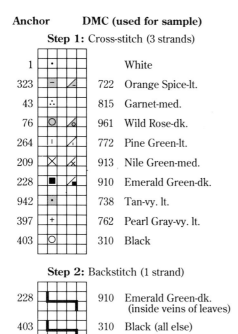

Anchor		DMC (used for sample)
Step 1: Cross-stitch (3 strands)		
1		White
323		722 Orange Spice-lt.
43		815 Garnet-med.
76		961 Wild Rose-dk.
264		772 Pine Green-lt.
209		913 Nile Green-med.
228		910 Emerald Green-dk.
942		738 Tan-vy. lt.
397		762 Pearl Gray-vy. lt.
403		310 Black

Step 2: Backstitch (1 strand)

228		910 Emerald Green-dk. (inside veins of leaves)
403		310 Black (all else)

Whatnot Box
Stitch Count : 52 x 52

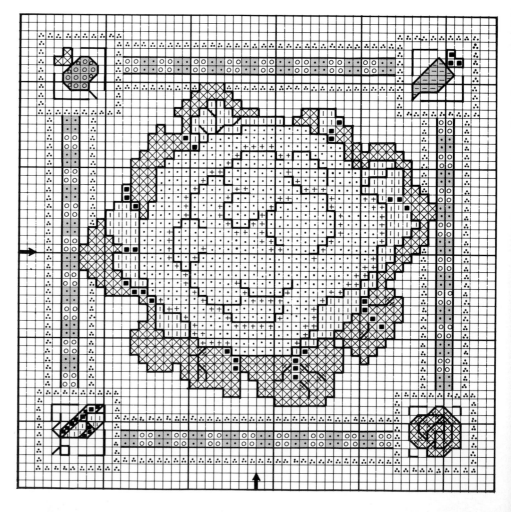

CRISP GREENS PLACEMAT

Stitched on ivory Aida 14 over one thread, the finished design size is 1⅜" x 9¼" for one side of the mat. The fabric was cut 20" x 16" for the complete mat. The design is taken from the graph on page 64. Begin stitching design with the garnet boxes 1¾" from short sides (carrots and radishes pointing toward the center of the placemat) and centered top to bottom. Rotate fabric and repeat design on opposite side.

FABRIC

FABRIC	DESIGN SIZES
Aida 11	1⅞" x 11⅞"
Aida 18	1⅛" x 7¼"
Hardanger 22	⅞" x 5⅞"

MATERIALS

Completed design
⅛ yard black fabric
Black sewing thread
Straight pins

DIRECTIONS

1. Trim the design fabric to 18" x 13" with the garnet boxes ¾" from short sides and 1¾" from long sides.

2. Cut and piece the black fabric into 65" x 1⅝" strip. Fold it in half lengthwise and press.

3. Pin the binding strip to the front of the design fabric and align raw edges, mitering corners if desired; where the binding strip ends meet, fold one end back ½" and overlap the other end (trim away excess fabric). Sew the binding strip and design fabric together ¼" from the raw edges. Fold the binding to the back of the design and hand-stitch together. Take care that the stitches don't show on the front (again mitering corners if desired).

Anchor		DMC (used for sample)	
	Step 1: Cross-stitch (3 strands)		
1			White
323		722	Orange Spice-lt.
43		815	Garnet-med.
76		961	Wild Rose-dk.
264		772	Pine Green-lt.
209		913	Nile Green-med.
942		738	Tan-vy. lt.
403		310	Black
	Step 2: Backstitch (1 strand)		
228		910	Emerald Green-dk. (inside lettuce)
403		310	Black (all else)

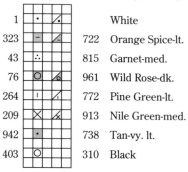

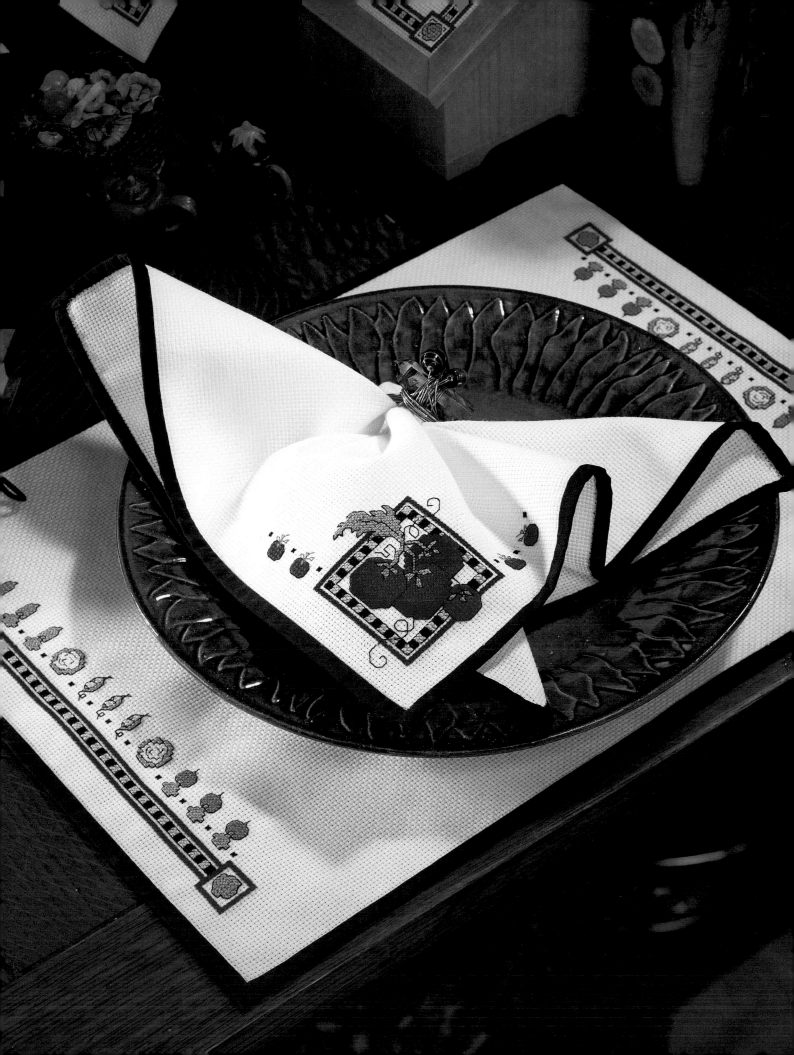

RIPENED CHAIR COVER

Stitched on ivory Aida 14 over one thread, the finished design size is 9⅜" x 5⅛'". The fabric was cut 24" x 11". The design was taken from the graph on page 64.

FABRIC   **DESIGN SIZES**
Aida 11   11⅞" x 6½"
Aida 18   7¼" x 4"
Hardanger 22   6" x 3¼"

MATERIALS
Completed design
½ yard of black fabric
⅝ yard of ivory fabric
¼ yard of ivory pre-quilted fabric
¼" cotton cord
Ivory and black sewing thread
Straight pins

DIRECTIONS
All seam allowances are ½".

1. Enlarge pattern on page 66 to 200 % (½" seam allowances included) on a photocopying machine. Using this pattern, cut one piece each from pre-quilted and ivory fabric.

2. Using pattern, cut design fabric with design centered.

3. Baste ivory piece to back of design fabric.

4. Cut and piece ivory fabric into 122" x 6" strip. With right sides facing, sew short sides together to form a loop. Fold in half lengthwise and press. Pin and baste 1" box pleats around loop to form pleated ruffle. Set aside.

5. Cut and piece black fabric into 80" x 1½" bias strip. Using strip and cord, make piping.

6. Baste piping to right of design fabric around sides and top.

7. With right sides facing, sew quilted backing to design unit around sides and top. Trim seam allowance, clip corners, and turn.

8. Starting on the pre-quilted side, baste remaining piping to bottom front of design unit, aligning raw edges and overlapping ends.

9. With right sides facing and raw edges aligned, baste and sew pleated ruffle to bottom of design unit, easing if necessary.

10. Press ruffle to hang down.

Anchor			DMC (used for sample)	
Step 1: Cross-stitch (3 strands)				
1	·	⁄		White
323	–		722	Orange Spice-lt.
324	∴		721	Orange Spice-med.
335	△	⁄	606	Orange Red-bright
47	▲	⁄	321	Christmas Red
43	∷		815	Garnet-med.
76	○	⁄	961	Wild Rose-dk.
42	✕		3350	Dusty Rose-dk.
264	ı	⁄	772	Pine Green-lt.
206	▢	⁄	955	Nile Green-lt.
209	✕	⁄	913	Nile Green-med.
228	■	⁄	910	Emerald Green-dk.
942	·	⁄	738	Tan-vy. lt.
403	○		310	Black

		DMC	
Step 2: Backstitch (1 strand)			
228		910	Emerald Green-dk. (inside veins of lettuce leaves)
403		310	Black (all else)

62

Crisp Greens Placemat   **Stitch count: 20 x 130**

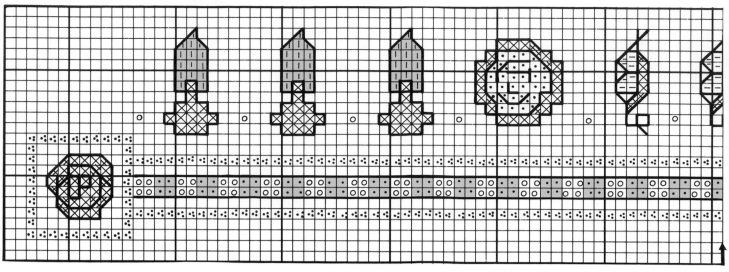

Ripened Chair Cover   **Stitch count: 131 x 72**

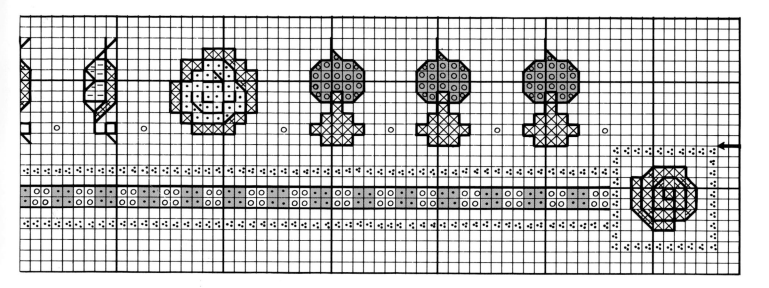

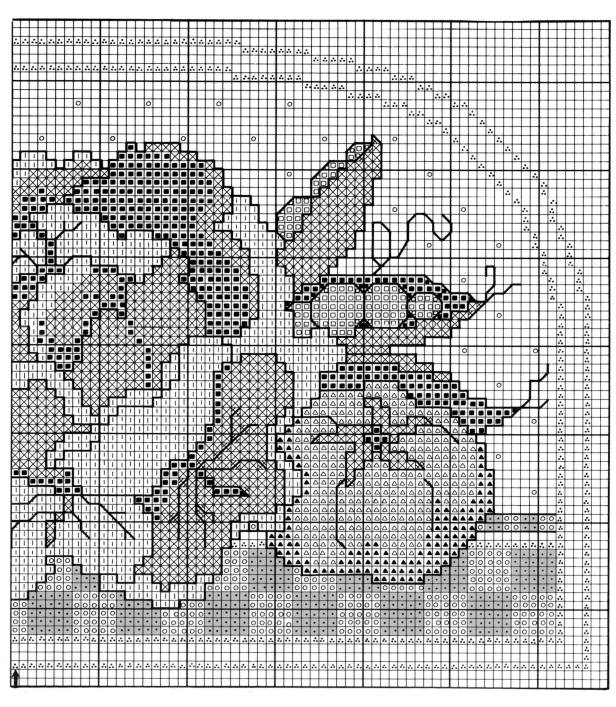

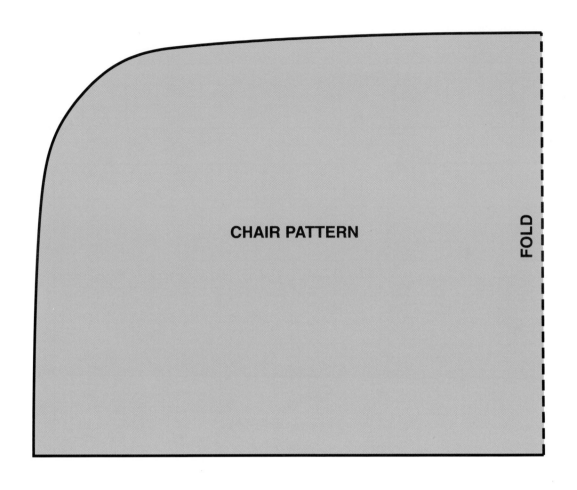

CHAIR PATTERN

FOLD

VEGGIE RUG

MATERIALS

2' x 3' tan ribbed floor rug

Black, red, green, yellow-green, orange, and medium and light mauve stencil paint

Stencil brushes (one for each color)

Hot stencil cutter

Eight 9" x 12" sheets of stencil plastic

One 9" x 12" glass sheet (edges taped)

Stencil adhesive

Masking tape

DIRECTIONS

1. Enlarge stencil to 150%, using an enlarging photocopy machine.

2. Tape stencil plastic sheets to the glass with the enlarged design between plastic and glass. Cut stencils (about one sheet per color), using the hot stencil cutter. Two stencil sheets may be taped together for the area needed for the yellow-green color. Be sure to mark on each stencil some surrounding reference areas (usually this is done with dotted lines—don't cut these areas out). Cut stencils for the following:

- ✂ checkerboard border corner
- ✂ checkerboard strip
- ✂ yellow-green areas for entire central vegetable design (two sheets taped together)
- ✂ green areas (two sheets taped together)
- ✂ orange and red areas
- ✂ dark and light pink areas

3. Place border design 1¾" from rug edges (excluding fringe). Border repeats itself around the rug. Centrally place vegetable cluster within the checkerboard border. Stencil adhesive is used on the back of a stencil to "stick" the stencil to the rug surface to prevent it from moving during the stenciling process.

4. Following instructions with the stencil paint, stencil the design, letting each color dry before painting the next. Brush the color from the stencil into the cutout area to achieve a crisp outline. Because the rug is ribbed, it takes a fair amount of effort to get the paint into the crevices. Paint in the following order:

- 🖌 border
- 🖌 yellow-green areas
- 🖌 green areas
- 🖌 red areas
- 🖌 orange areas
- 🖌 dark and light pink areas

68

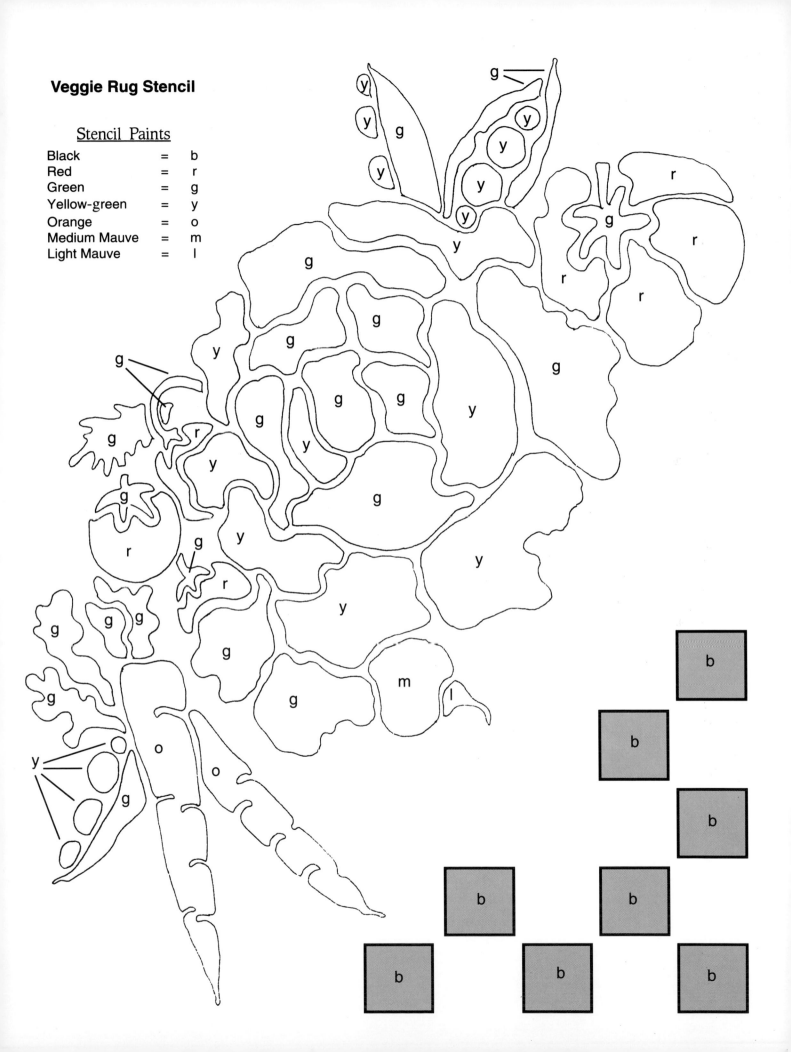

Veggie Rug Stencil

Stencil Paints

Black	=	b
Red	=	r
Green	=	g
Yellow-green	=	y
Orange	=	o
Medium Mauve	=	m
Light Mauve	=	l

DINING ROOM

Better is a dinner of herbs where love is...

Gospel of St. Matthew

CARNATION SAMPLER

Stitched on light mocha Cashel linen 28 over two threads, the finished design size is 12½" x 9". The fabric was cut 19" x 15".

FABRIC	DESIGN SIZES
Aida 11	15⅞" x 11½"
Aida 14	12½" x 9"
Aida 18	9¾" x 7"
Hardanger 22	8" x 5¾"

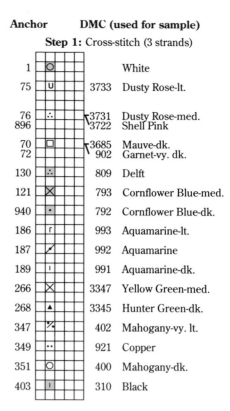

Anchor		DMC (used for sample)	
		Step 1: Cross-stitch (3 strands)	
1	○		White
75	U	3733	Dusty Rose-lt.
76	∴	3731	Dusty Rose-med.
896		3722	Shell Pink
70	□	3685	Mauve-dk.
72		902	Garnet-vy. dk.
130	∴	809	Delft
121	✕	793	Cornflower Blue-med.
940	·	792	Cornflower Blue-dk.
186	ſ	993	Aquamarine-lt.
187	╱	992	Aquamarine
189	ı	991	Aquamarine-dk.
266	✕	3347	Yellow Green-med.
268	▲	3345	Hunter Green-dk.
347	╱	402	Mahogany-vy. lt.
349	∵	921	Copper
351	○	400	Mahogany-dk.
403	ı	310	Black

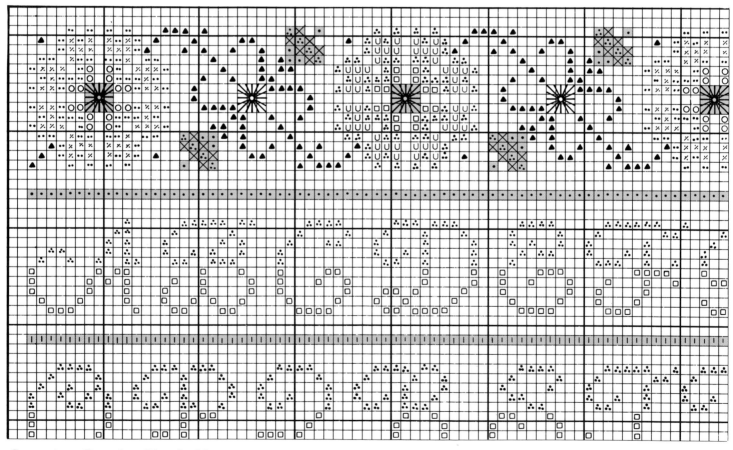

Carnation Sampler (Top Left)   **Stitch count: 175 x 126**

Step 2: Backstitch (1 strand)

1   White (birds' eyes)

Step 3: Satin Stitch (4 strands)

1   White

Step 4: Algerian Eye Stitch (2 strands)

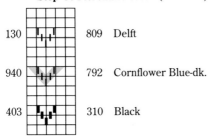

| 268 | | 3345 | Hunter Green-dk. (leaves) |
| 403 | | 310 | Black (flower centers) |

Step 5: Florentine Stitch (4 strands)

130		809	Delft
940		792	Cornflower Blue-dk.
403		310	Black

SPRIG NAPKIN

Stitched 1¾" from one corner on light mocha Cashel linen 28 over two threads, the finished design size is 1¼" x ¾". The fabric was cut 18" x 18". The design was taken from the carnation sprig which follows the letter Z of the alphabet on the Carnation Sampler graph. Edges are folded under ¼" and ¼" again (mitering corners if desired), pressed and topstitched with matching thread. **Stitch count: 21 x 10**

FABRIC	DESIGN SIZES
Aida 11	1⅞" x ⅞"
Aida 14	1½" x ¾"
Aida 18	1⅛" x ½"
Hardanger 22	1" x ½"

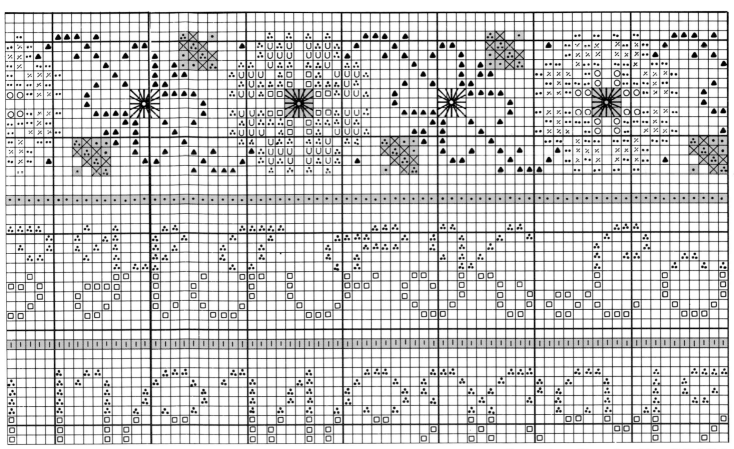

Carnation Sampler Top (Middle)

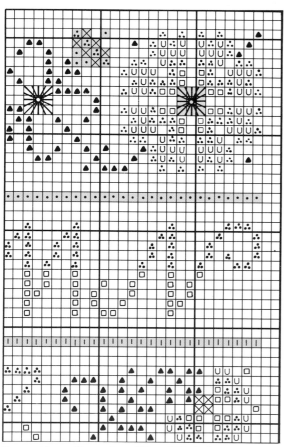

Carnation Sampler (Top Right)

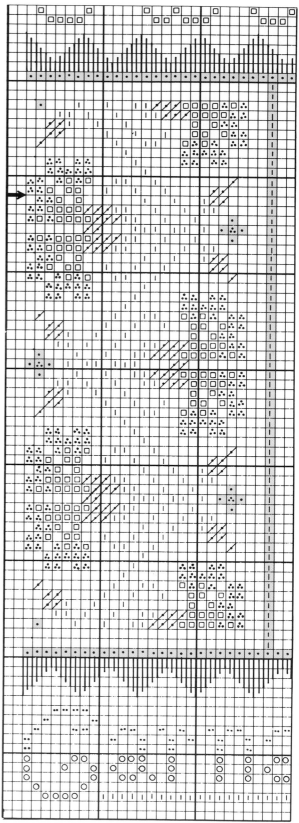

Carnation Sampler (Bottom Left)

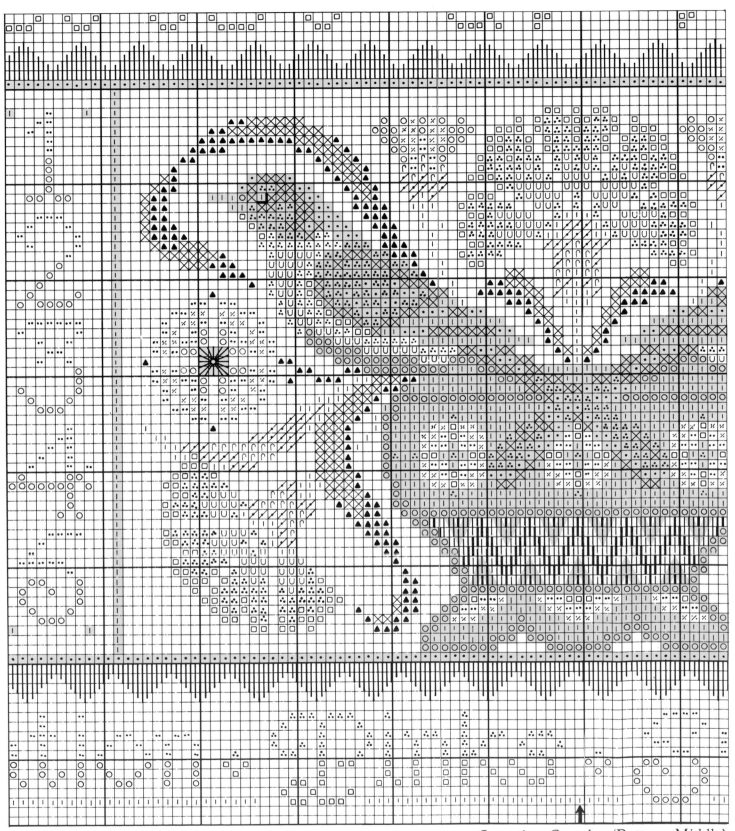

Carnation Sampler (Bottom Middle)

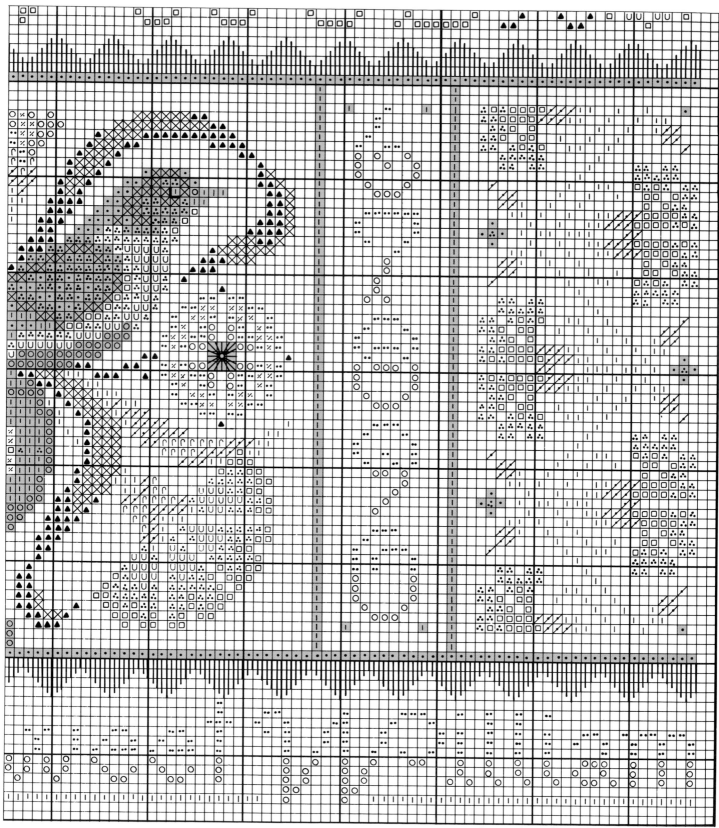

Carnation Sampler (Bottom Right)

Stitched on light mocha Cashel linen 28 over two threads, the finished design size is 6½" x 4⅛". The fabric was cut 11" x 8". The design was taken from the center vase with carnations and birds on the Carnation Sampler graph.

FABRIC
FABRIC	DESIGN SIZES
Aida 11	8¼" x 5⅛"
Aida 14	6½" x 4⅛"
Aida 18	5" x 3⅛"
Hardanger 22	4⅛" x 2⅝"

Stitch count: 91 x 57

MATERIALS
Completed design
11½" x 23" white-washed wall clock with an
    8⅜" x 5¾" design area
8½" x 5⅞" piece of foam core or heavyweight
    cardboard
8½" x 5⅞" piece of fleece
Thick fabric glue

DIRECTIONS
1. Glue fleece to foam core.

2. Place design right side up over fleece with design 1" from sides and 1⅝" from bottom. Pull fabric edges to back of fleece piece and glue.

3. Insert design piece into opening at base of clock and push it to the front of clock until it is even with the clock front.

PRETTY PLACEMAT

Stitched on light mocha Cashel linen 28 over two threads, the finished design size is 17⅛" x 1⅛". The fabric was cut 5" x 22". The design is taken from the carnation border that runs across the top of the Carnation Sampler graph.

FABRIC	DESIGN SIZES
Aida 11	21¾" x 1⅜"
Aida 14	17⅛" x 1⅛"
Aida 18	13¼" x ⅞"
Hardanger 22	10⅞" x ⅝"

Stitch count: 239 x 15

MATERIALS
Completed design
⅝ yard of light tan damask fabric and matching
    thread
3"-high tan tassel

DIRECTIONS
All seam allowances are ½".

1. Enlarge pattern from page 78 to 250% on an enlarging photocopy machine (½" seam allowances are included). Using this pattern, cut two pieces from damask fabric.

2. Trim design fabric to 2½" x 19¾" with design centered. Turn long sides under ½" and press.

3. Pin and baste design fabric (right side up) on the right side of one of the damask pieces and 1¼" from the side opposite the acute point.

4. Edge-stitch design fabric to damask fabric.

5. Tack tassel to acute point.

6. With right sides facing, pin design piece to remaining damask piece and sew around all sides, leaving a 6" opening along one side. Trim corners and turn right side out. Slipstitch opening closed.

PRETTY PLACEMAT PATTERN

Napkin Flower Ring

Stitched on light mocha Cashel linen 28 over two threads, the finished design size is 1¾" x 2". The fabric was cut 5½" x 7". The design was taken from the center carnation in the vase on the Carnation Sampler graph.

FABRIC	DESIGN SIZES
Aida 11	2¼" x 2½"
Aida 14	1¾" x 2"
Aida 18	1⅜" x 1½"
Hardanger 22	1⅛" x 1¼"

Stitch count: 25 x 27

MATERIALS
Completed design
2¼" x 6" piece of fleece
DMC 6-stranded floss #3782
⅝" tan shank button and matching thread

DIRECTIONS
All seam allowances are ½".

1. Matching raw edges of long sides with right side facing, sew together. Trim seam.

2. Turn right side out, press, and insert and center fleece into design piece.

3. Turn ends in ½" and trim.

4. Using three lengths of floss (six strands in each length), braid for 3". Secure each end with small tight knot.

5. Fold braid in half to form loop. Insert raw ends into open seam on right side of design piece (design facing you), center braided loop, and edge-stitch closed.

6. Center and tack button at seam on left side of design piece.

7. Wrap napkin ring around napkin and button closed. Note: Napkin ring can be stored open and flat.

Trimming Candles

Stitched on light mocha Cashel linen 28 over two threads, the finished design size is 5⅞" x 1⅝". The fabric was cut 8" x 14". The design was taken from the vertical carnation borders that run along the sides of the Carnation Sampler graph.

FABRIC	DESIGN SIZES
Aida 11	7½" x 2⅛"
Aida 14	5⅞" x 1⅝"
Aida 18	4⅝" x 1¼"
Hardanger 22	3¾" x 1"

Stitch count: 83 x 23

MATERIALS
Completed design
2¼" x 9¾" piece of fleece
⅜" x 2¼" of tan velcro and matching thread
2¾" rose candle (height is variable)

DIRECTIONS
All seam allowances are ½".

1. Trim design fabric to 5½" x 10¾" with design centered.

2. Matching raw edges of long sides with right side facing, sew together. Trim seam.

3. Turn right side out, press, and insert and center fleece into design piece.

4. Turn ends in ½" and edge-stitch.

5. Pin velcro to the ends of the design piece with the "hook" section at left side on the front of the design piece and the "felted" section at the right side but on the back of the design piece. Sew velcro in position.

6. Place around base of candle.

We bow our heads and close

our eyes and say a little prayer,

we thank our father graciously

for blessings we all share.

Anna Johnson

BATHROOM

*It takes a heap o' livin' in a house t'
make it "home" — and that's the truth.*

Flora Amussen Benson

SEASCAPE

Stitched on baby pink Aida 18 over one thread, the finished design size is 8" x 8⅛". The fabric was cut 14" x 15".

FABRIC
Aida 11
Aida 14
Hardanger 22

DESIGN SIZES
13⅛" x 13⅜"
10¼" x 10½"
6½" x 6⅝"

Seascape (Top Left)

Stitch count: 143 x 147

Anchor		DMC (used for sample)	
		Step 1: Cross-stitch (3 strands)	
1	·		White
386	–	746	Off White
880	I	948	Peach-vy. lt.
4146	+	754	Peach-lt.
881	△	945	Peach Beige
892	/	3770	Peach Pecan-vy. lt.
366	▽	951	Peach Pecan-lt.

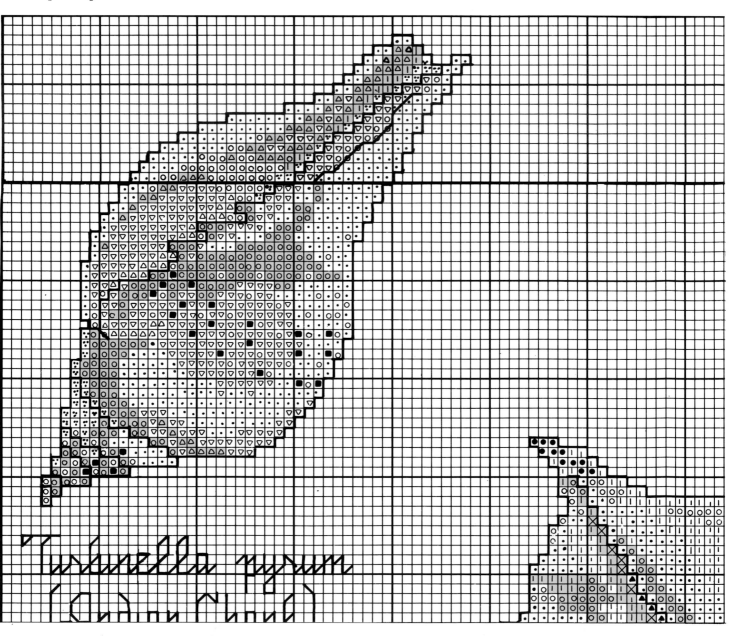

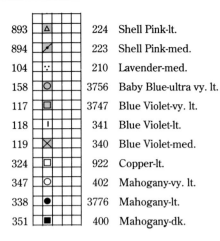

893	△	224	Shell Pink-lt.
894	◪	223	Shell Pink-med.
104	⬚	210	Lavender-med.
158	◯	3756	Baby Blue-ultra vy. lt.
117	▢	3747	Blue Violet-vy. lt.
118	I	341	Blue Violet-lt.
119	✕	340	Blue Violet-med.
324	▢	922	Copper-lt.
347	○	402	Mahogany-vy. lt.
338	●	3776	Mahogany-lt.
351	■	400	Mahogany-dk.

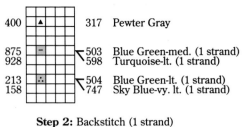

400	▲		317	Pewter Gray
875	–	503	Blue Green-med. (1 strand)
928		598	Turquoise-lt. (1 strand)
213	∴	504	Blue Green-lt. (1 strand)
158		747	Sky Blue-vy. lt. (1 strand)

Step 2: Backstitch (1 strand)

| 896 | ⌐ | 3722 | Shell Pink |

Seascape (Top Right)

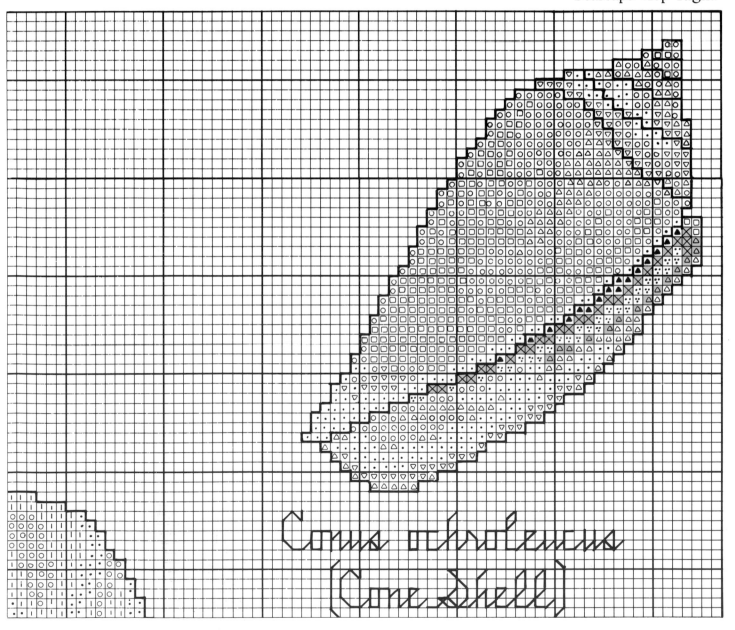

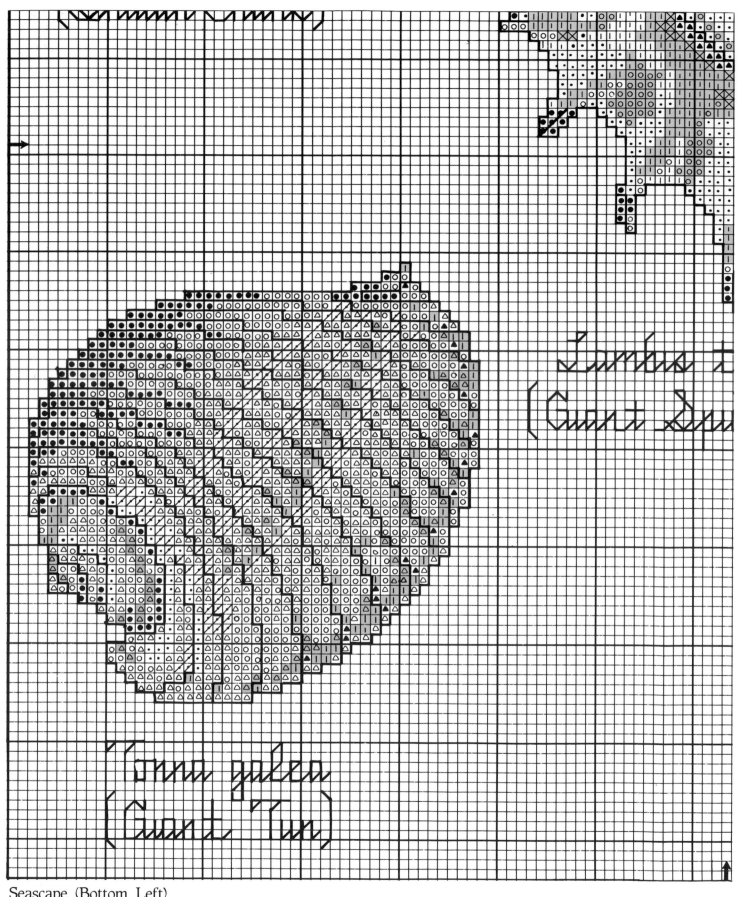

Seascape (Bottom Left)

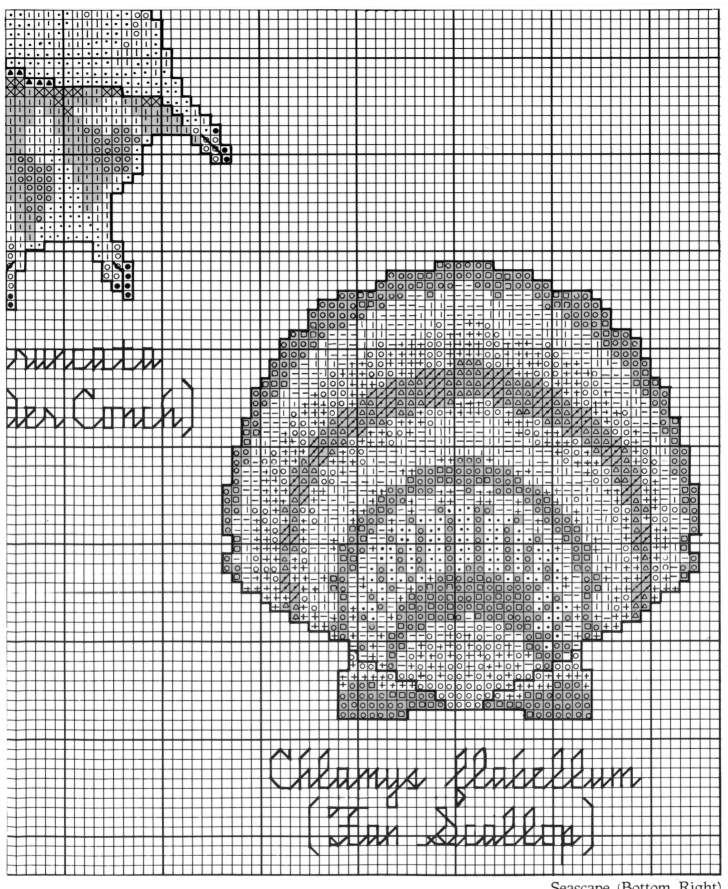

Seascape (Bottom Right)

SHELLED BASKET

Stitched on baby pink Aida 14 over one thread, the finished design size is 19⅞" x 3⅜". The fabric was cut 11" x basket perimeter plus 8". Use code on page 84.

FABRIC   **DESIGN SIZES**
Aida 11   25⅜" x 4⅜"
Aida 18   15½" x 2⅝"
Hardanger 22   12⅝" x 2⅛"

MATERIALS
Completed design
½ yard of pink satin fabric and matching thread
Fleece
Two 2½" x ¾" Velcro strips
Wicker basket with minimum dimensions of
    21" wide x 7" high
Pink stencil paint, stencil brush and cloth rag

DIRECTIONS
1. Trim design fabric to 5⅛ x basket perimeter plus 4" with design centered. Additional Aida pieces may need to be added to each end of the design fabric in

Shells and Sea (Left)   **Stitch count: 279 x 48**

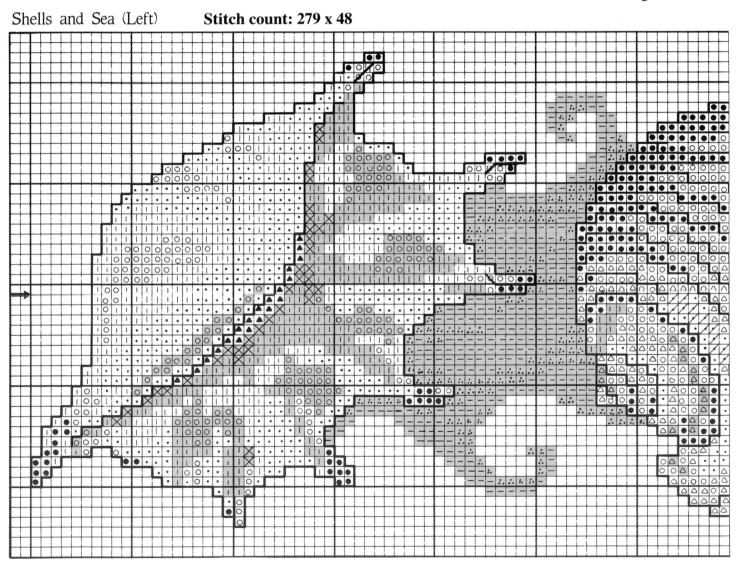

order for the fabric strip to fit completely around the basket.

2. Using design fabric as pattern, cut fleece. Trim 1" from one short edge and ⅛" from one long edge.

3. For backing, cut satin fabric 6⅛" x basket perimeter plus 4" (piecing if necessary).

4. With right sides facing and using ½" seam allowance, sew long edges of design fabric and backing. Turn (seam lines roll toward front of design fabric with satin backing forming a ½" edging).

5. Turn each short end under ½" and press.

6. Insert fleece into design piece tube. Slipstich each end closed and press.

7. Topstitch adjacent to satin edging.

8. Sew hook-side pieces of Velcro to back of right-hand side of design piece, aligning the long sides of the Velcro strips adjacent to the long sides of the design piece at the top and bottom edges. Sew felted side of Velcro to front of left-hand side of the the design piece with the long sides adjacent to the long sides of the design piece at top and bottom edges.

9. Wrap design unit tightly around basket, overlapping the short ends of design unit at the back of the basket.

Shells and Sea (Left Middle)

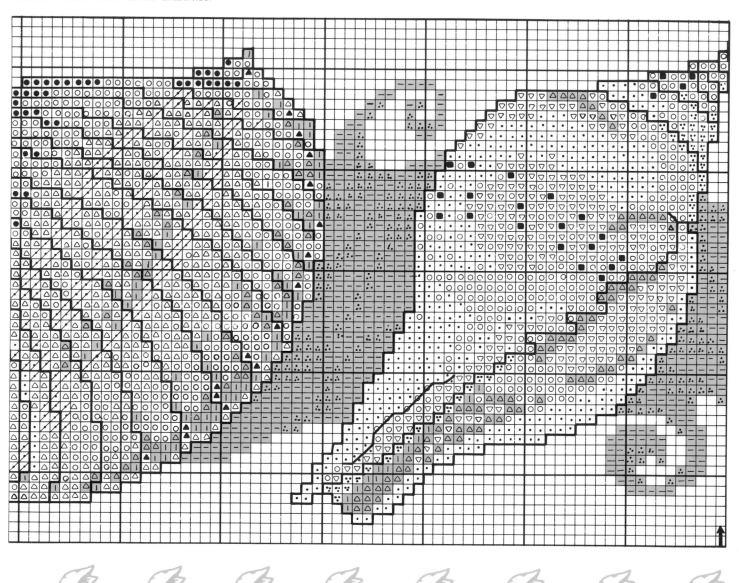

SHOWERED WITH SHELLS

Stitched on baby pink Aida 14 over one thread, the finished design size is 13⅛" x 3⅜". The fabric was cut 37" x 8". The design is taken from the Shells and Sea graph omitting the far right giant spider conch shell and the water motif between it and the adjacent cone shell. See Fig. Y on page 93 for design placement for either left or right side tieback. Use code on page 84. **Stitch count: 183 x 48**

FABRIC

FABRIC	DESIGN SIZES
Aida 11	16⅝" x 4⅜"
Aida 18	10⅛" x 2⅝"
Hardanger 22	8⅜" x 2⅛"

MATERIALS

Completed design
½ yard of shell pink fabric and matching thread
5½" x 32" piece of fleece
Decorative tieback hook

DIRECTIONS

All seam allowances are ½".

1. Using the fleece piece as a pattern, cut backing from shell pink fabric. Cut two 3" x 5½", one 3" x 33", and one 3" x 39" strips from shell pink fabric.

Shells and Sea (Right Middle)

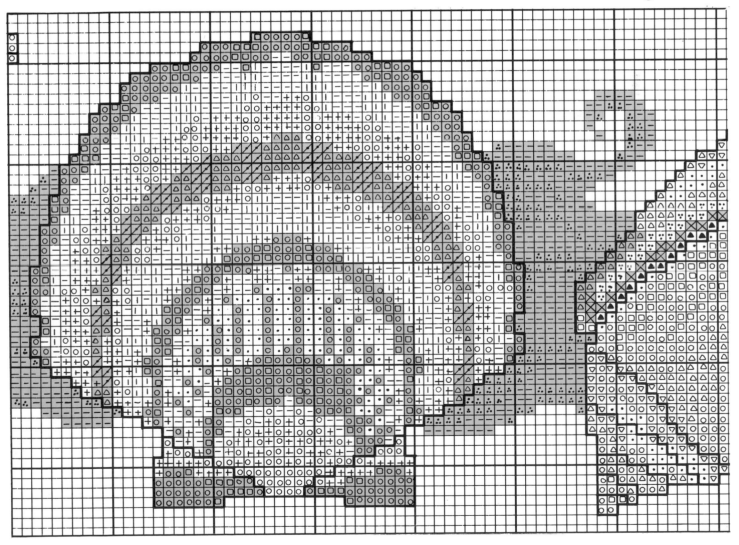

2. Trim 1¼" from top and bottom edges and 2½" from each side of design fabric. Final dimensions should be 5½" x 32".

3. Pin and baste the following layers: design fabric (face up), fleece, backing (face down).

4. Fold and press the two short strips in half lengthwise. Match the raw edges of one short strip to a short side of the design piece front and sew together. Turn folded edge to back and slipstitch in place. Repeat for other side, using remaining short strip.

5. Fold and press the two long strips in half lengthwise.

6. Fold and press the ends of the shorter strip under ½". Match the raw edges of the shorter strip to the bottom edge of the design piece front and sew together. Turn folded edge to back and slipstitch in place.

7. Fold and press the ends of the remaining strip under ½". Match the raw edges to the top edge of the design piece front, leaving 3" free at each end. Turn folded edge to back and slipstitch in place, including tab ends.

8. Fold 1½" of tab ends to back and tack in place.

9. Attach tieback hook to bathroom wall. Slip tab ends onto hook, gathering shower curtain within tieback.

Shells and Sea (Right)

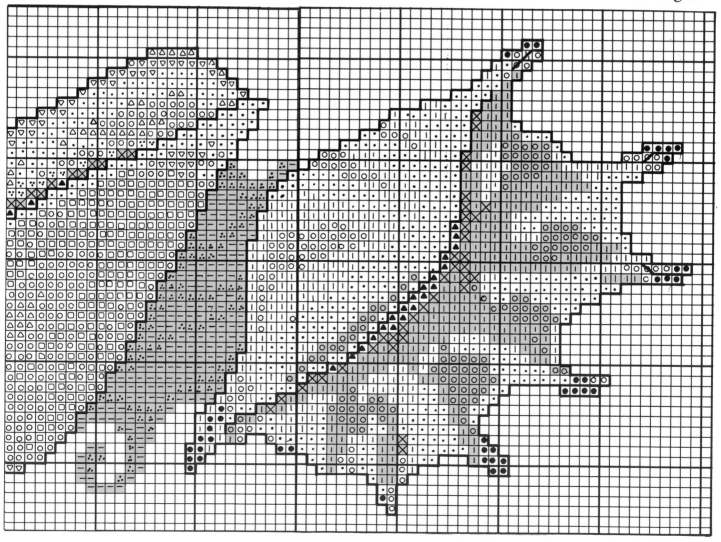

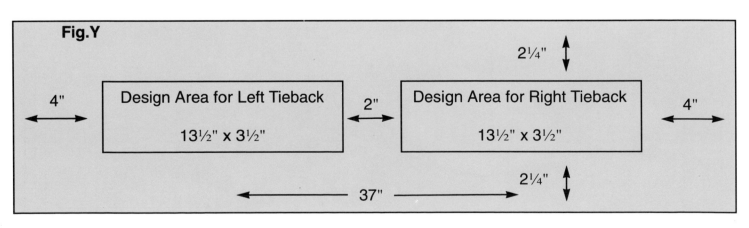

Fig.Y

2¼" ↕

4" ↔ | Design Area for Left Tieback
13½" x 3½" | 2" ↔ | Design Area for Right Tieback
13½" x 3½" | 4" ↔

2¼" ↕

← 37" →

Stitched on baby pink Aida 14 over one thread, the finished design size is 2¾" x 3¼". The fabric was cut 6" x 8".

FABRIC   **DESIGN SIZES**

Aida 11	3½" x 4⅛"
Aida 18	2⅛" x 2½"
Hardanger 22	1¾" x 2"

MATERIALS
Completed design
⅜ yard of shell pink fabric and matching thread
4" x 5" piece of fleece
16" of ⅜" cotton cording
Two 4" x 5" pieces of medium-weight cardboard
1 yard of ½"-wide shell pink satin ribbon
Thick fabric glue

DIRECTIONS

1. Trace oval pattern on page 98. Place pattern over back of design with design centered and lightly trace around cutting line of pattern. Cut design fabric on traced line. Using same pattern, cut one oval from shell pink fabric for the backing.

2. Using pattern, trace and cut fleece and both cardboard pieces on seam line.

3. Glue fleece to one cardboard piece.

4. Center design fabric over fleece piece with design centered. Pull raw edges to back and glue.

5. Cut and piece shell pink fabric to make 1⅝" x 16" bias strip. Using bias strip and cording, make piping.

Anchor		DMC (used for sample)

Step 1: Cross-stitch (3 strands)

1	·	White
158	O	3756 Baby Blue-ultra vy. lt.
117	□	3747 Blue Violet-vy. lt.
118	X	340 Blue Violet-med.

347	O	402 Mahogany-vy. lt.
338	●	3776 Mahogany-lt.
351	■	400 Mahogany-dk.
401	△	413 Pewter Gray-dk.
875 / 928	−	503 Blue Green-med. (1 strand) / 598 Turquoise-lt. (1 strand)

| 213 / 158 | ∴ | 504 Blue Green-lt. (1 strand) / 747 Sky Blue-vy. lt. (1 strand) |

Step 2: Backstitch (1 strand)

| 896 | — | 3722 Shell Pink |

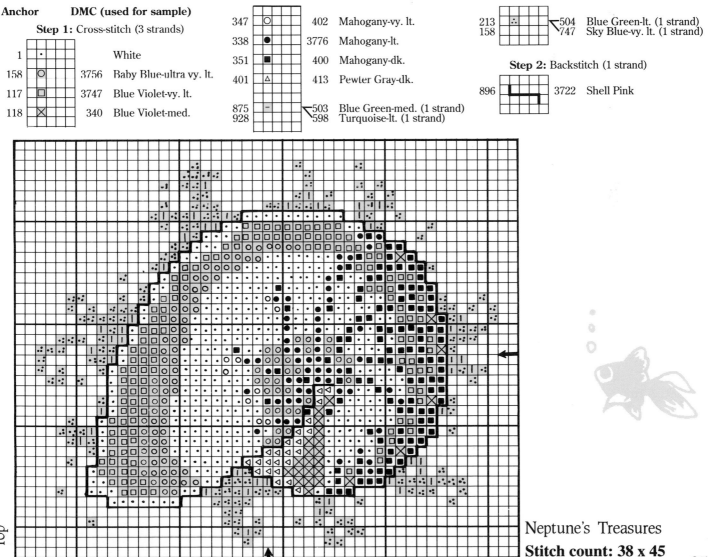

Top

Neptune's Treasures
Stitch count: 38 x 45

6. Glue piping around back edge of design piece, overlapping ends at one side.

7. Fold ribbon in half forming a point (Fig. XX on page 99). Glue ribbon to back of design piece with the point extending beyond bottom of design piece and the streamers extending at top.

8. Center remaining cardboard over wrong side of backing fabric.

9. Glue backing to wrong side of design piece, weighted with a book or covered brick until dry.

10. Tie finished design piece to handle of basket, adjusting size of bow to fit basket size. Decoratively trim ribbon ends.

TOWEL OFF

Stitched on baby pink Aida 14 over one thread, the finished design size is 2⅝" x 3⅜" for the New Guinea Stromb design and 2¾" x 3⅝" for the Dwarf Olive design. The fabric for each was cut 6" x 8". The designs were taken from the graphs on pages 98 and 99.

New Guinea Stromb

FABRIC	DESIGN SIZES
Aida 11	3¼" x 4¼"
Aida 18	2" x 2⅝"
Hardanger 22	1⅝" x 2⅛"

Dwarf Olive

FABRIC	DESIGN SIZES
Aida 11	3½" x 4½"
Aida 18	2⅛" x 2¾"
Hardanger 22	1¾" x 2¼"

MATERIALS
Completed design
⅜ yard of shell pink fabric and matching thread
4" x 5" piece of fleece
16" of ⅜" cotton cording
15½" x 29½" light peach terry guest towel

DIRECTIONS
1. For each towel, trace oval pattern on page 98. Place pattern over back of design with design centered and lightly trace around cutting line of pattern. Cut design fabric on traced line.

2. Using pattern, cut fleece on seam line.

3. Cut and piece shell pink fabric to make 1⅜" x 16" bias strip. Using fabric strip and cording, make piping.

4. With raw edges matching, baste and sew piping to right side of design fabric, overlapping ends at one side. Turn raw edges to back and press.

5. Place fleece at back of design piece beneath the raw edges.

6. Pin design piece face up on towel front ⅜" from decoratively woven border and centered side to side. Stitch between design fabric and piping.

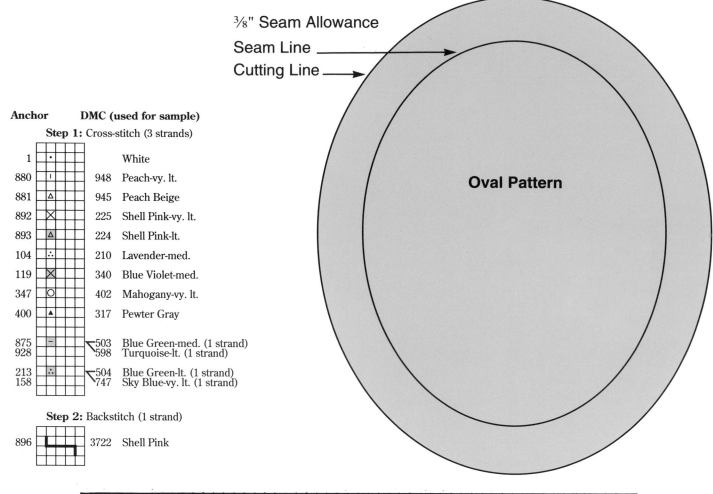

³⁄₈" Seam Allowance

Seam Line

Cutting Line

Oval Pattern

Anchor   DMC (used for sample)

Step 1: Cross-stitch (3 strands)

Anchor		DMC	
1	·		White
880	I	948	Peach-vy. lt.
881	△	945	Peach Beige
892	✕	225	Shell Pink-vy. lt.
893	◸	224	Shell Pink-lt.
104	⋰	210	Lavender-med.
119	✕	340	Blue Violet-med.
347	○	402	Mahogany-vy. lt.
400	▲	317	Pewter Gray
875 928	−	503 598	Blue Green-med. (1 strand) Turquoise-lt. (1 strand)
213 158	⋰	504 747	Blue Green-lt. (1 strand) Sky Blue-vy. lt. (1 strand)

Step 2: Backstitch (1 strand)

896	⌐	3722	Shell Pink

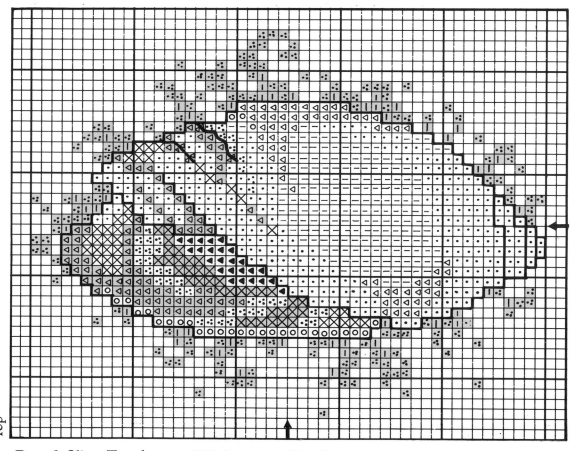

Top

98   Dwarf Olive Towel   **Stitch count: 38 x 50**

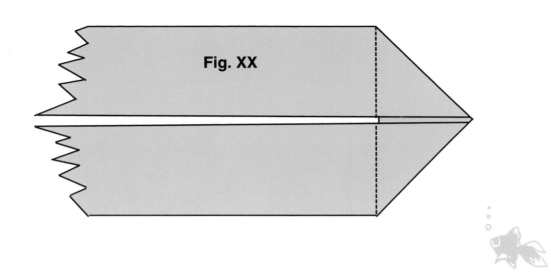

Fig. XX

New Guinea Stromb Towel   **Stitch count: 36 x 47**

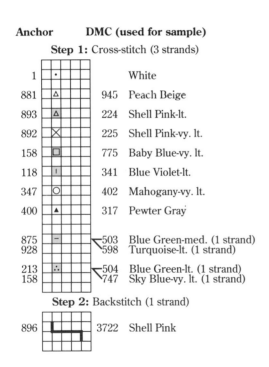

Anchor   DMC (used for sample)

Step 1: Cross-stitch (3 strands)

1	·	White
881	△	945 Peach Beige
893	▲	224 Shell Pink-lt.
892	✕	225 Shell Pink-vy. lt.
158	▢	775 Baby Blue-vy. lt.
118	I	341 Blue Violet-lt.
347	○	402 Mahogany-vy. lt.
400	▲	317 Pewter Gray
875	−	503 Blue Green-med. (1 strand)
928		598 Turquoise-lt. (1 strand)
213	∴	504 Blue Green-lt. (1 strand)
158		747 Sky Blue-vy. lt. (1 strand)

Step 2: Backstitch (1 strand)

896		3722 Shell Pink

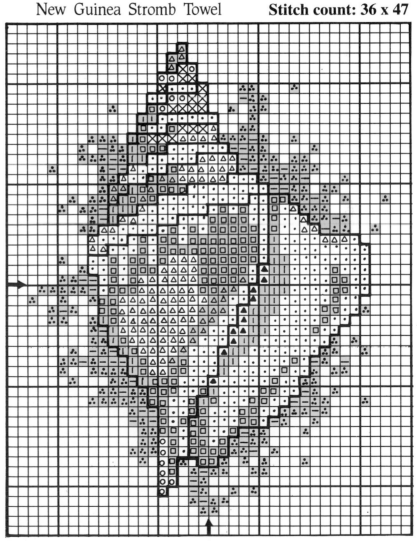

99

MASTER BEDROOM

A thing of beauty is a joy
forever:
Its loveliness increases;
it will never
Pass into nothingness, but still
will keep
A bower quiet for us, and a
sleep
Full of sweet dreams.

John Keats

SUITE PANSY COLLAGE

The collage is stitched on white Aida14 over one thread. The fabric was cut from ¾ yard to 8" x 10" for the Upright Pansy Plant, 8" x 17 ⅜" for the Horizontal Pansy Border, 14" x 14" for the Pansies in Vase, 7" x 14" for the Vertical Pansy Border, 8" x 8" for the Pansy-N-Ivy Circle and 3½" x 4" for the Pansy-n-Ivy Corners.

Upright Pansy Plant

FABRIC	DESIGN SIZES
Aida 11	4⅞" x 7⅜"
Aida 14	3⅞" x 5¾"
Aida 18	3" x 4½"
Hardanger 22	2½" x 3⅝"

Horizontal Pansy Border

FABRIC	DESIGN SIZES
Aida 11	16½" x 5"
Aida 14	13" x 3⅞"
Aida 18	10⅛" x 3"
Hardanger 22	8¼" x 2½"

Pansies in Vase

FABRIC	DESIGN SIZES
Aida 11	12⅛" x 11¾"
Aida 14	9½" x 9¼"
Aida 18	7⅜" x 7⅛"
Hardanger 22	6" x 5⅞"

Vertical Pansy Border

FABRIC	DESIGN SIZES
Aida 11	2⅞" x 12⅛"
Aida 14	2¼" x 9½"
Aida 18	1¾" x 7⅜"
Hardanger 22	1⅜" x 6"

Pansy-n-Ivy Circle

FABRIC	DESIGN SIZES
Aida 11	4⅞" x 4¾"
Aida 14	3⅞" x 3¾"
Aida 18	3" x 2⅞"
Hardanger 22	2½" x 2⅞"

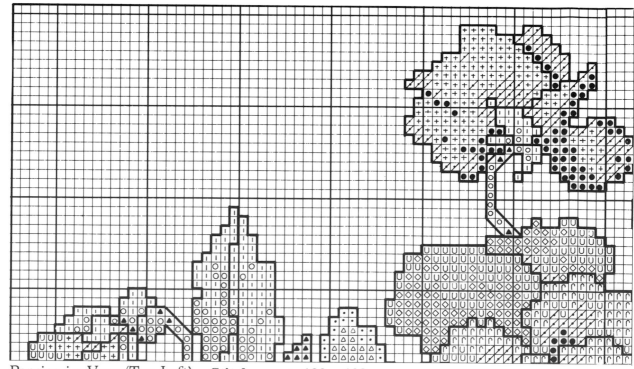

Pansies in Vase (Top Left)   **Stitch count: 133 x 129**

Pansy-n-Ivy Corners

FABRIC	DESIGN SIZES
Aida 11	4⅜" x 4⅜"
Aida 14	3⅜" x 3⅜"
Aida 18	2⅝" x 2⅝"
Hardanger 22	2⅛" x 2⅛"

MATERIALS

Completed designs
½ yard of pale periwinkle blue fabric
1 yard of fleece
6¾ yards of ⅜"-wide periwinkle blue grosgrain
 ribbon
½ sheet of ⅜" plywood
One sheet medium sandpaper (#100)
Double-stick tape
Sawtooth hanger
Lightweight staple gun and ¼" staples
Hot glue gun and glue

DIRECTIONS

1. Center and stitch personal monogram in Pansy-n-Ivy Corner design fabric (page 113), using large alphabet for surname and small alphabet for remaining letters.

2. Cut fleece into seven pieces (one each: 6" x 8", 6" x 15 ⅜", 12" x 12", 5" x 12", 6" x 6", 5½" x 6", and 18" x 21½").

3. Cut plywood into seven pieces (one each: 4" x 6", 4" x 13⅜", 10" x 10", 3" x 10", 4" x 4", 3½" x 4", and 16" x 19½"). Sand edges.

4. Place strips of double-stick tape around sides and top of each plywood piece.

5. Matching each plywood piece with its respective piece of fleece (fleece dimensions are 1" bigger on all sides than its plywood piece) and with the tape-side down, center each plywood piece over fleece. Press fleece onto sides of plywood and trim away excess fleece. Repeat for remaining plywood and fleece pieces.

6. Center each design fabric over its respective fleece and plywood piece; firmly pull fabric edges to back of plywood and glue.

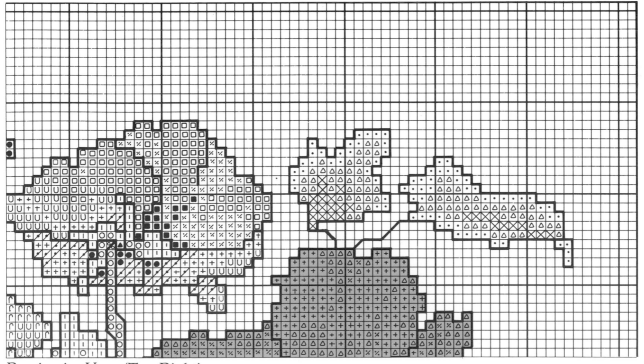

Pansies in Vase (Top Right)

103

Pansies in Vase (Bottom Left)

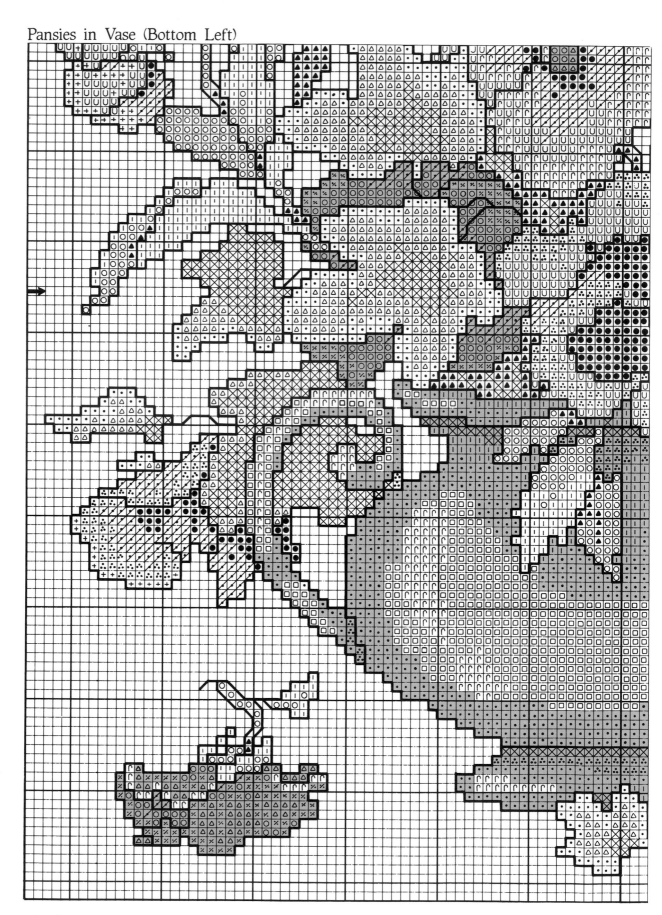

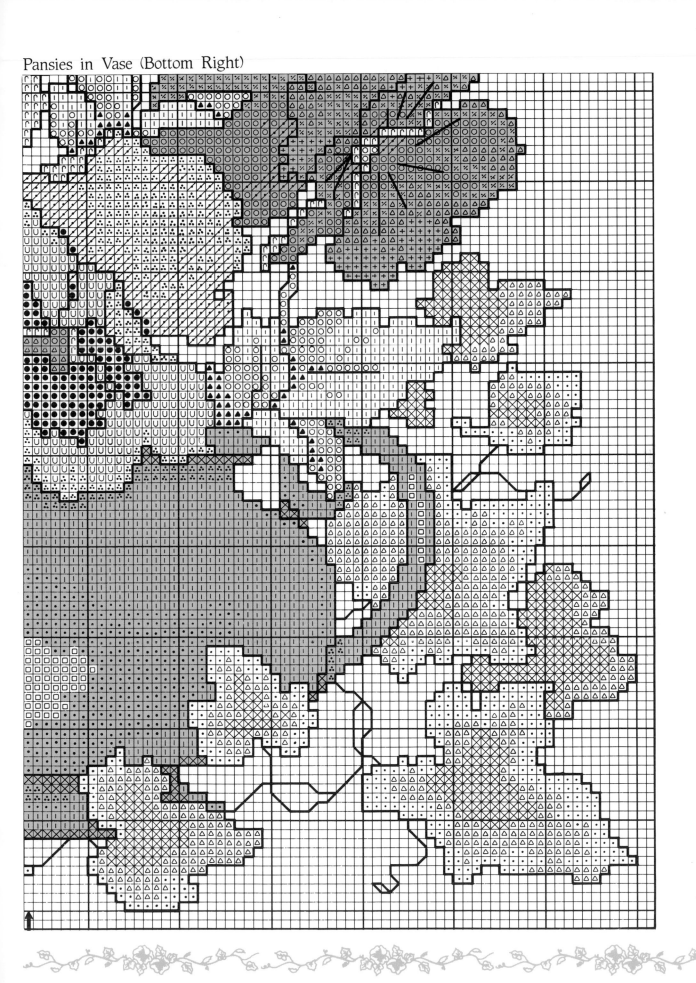

7. Cut blue fabric 19" x 22½". Center blue fabric over fleece and plywood; firmly pull edges to back of plywood and glue.

8. Beginning and overlapping at center bottom, carefully glue ribbon around sides of each design piece and blue-fabric piece. Let dry.

9. Arrange design pieces on blue-fabric piece (Fig. X) with ⅝" outer margin and approximately ¼" between design pieces.

10. Carefully lift up Pansies in Vase design piece without disturbing other design pieces. Staple area beneath design piece with several staples (this is to prevent a somewhat heavy design piece from pulling blue fabric forward, but no staples should show when design piece is replaced). Place this design piece back in position. Repeat for each design piece.

11. Hot-glue each design piece in place.

12. Attach sawtooth hanger to top center back of completed Suite Pansy Collage.

Fig. X

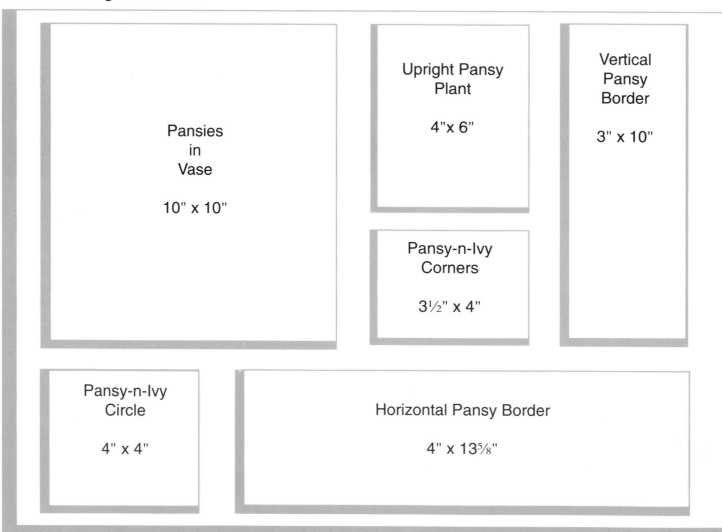

Pansies
in
Vase

10" x 10"

Upright Pansy
Plant

4"x 6"

Vertical
Pansy
Border

3" x 10"

Pansy-n-Ivy
Corners

3½" x 4"

Pansy-n-Ivy
Circle

4" x 4"

Horizontal Pansy Border

4" x 13⅝"

PANSY PLANT BED CADDY

Stitched on white Aida 14 inset over one thread, the finished design size is 3⅞" x 5¾". The fabric was cut 7⅛" x 7⅛" and trimmed with 2¼"-wide Battenberg lace. The design is taken from the Upright Pansy Plant graph on page 119.

FABRIC	DESIGN SIZES
Aida 11	4⅞" x 7⅜"
Aida 18	3" x 4½"
Hardanger 22	2¼" x 3⅝"

Stitch count: 54 x 81

MATERIALS

Completed design insert on 11½" x 12½" premade white bed caddy
¾ yard of 1¼"-wide white double-edged lace with white ribbon through central beading
1 yard of 1½"-wide white satin French wire ribbon

DIRECTIONS

1. Tack double-edged lace to front of caddy at seam between Aida and Battenberg-lace trim, folding ends back and mitering corners.

2. Tic ribbon into bow with loops 3" in length. Tack bow to center top of caddy, let ends trail into pocket area, and tack in place.

IVY HANGER

Stitched ¼" from one corner on white Aida 14 over one thread, the finished design size is 2⅛" x 2⅛". The fabric was cut 3¼" x 3¼" and trimmed with 1 ¾"-wide Battenberg lace. The design was taken from the Pansy-n-Ivy Corners (ivy only) graph on page113.

FABRIC	DESIGN SIZES
Aida 11	2¾" x 2¾"
Aida 18	1⅝" x 1⅝"
Hardanger 22	1⅜" x 1⅜"

Stitch count: 30 x 30

MATERIALS

Completed design
White lace-trimmed padded hanger
White sewing thread
12" of ⅝"-wide blue-green satin ribbon
16" of 1"-wide variegated lavender French wire ribbon
20" of 1½"-wide white satin French wire ribbon

DIRECTIONS

1. Make ¼" slit in design fabric 1¼" toward center from the corner opposite the stitched design and insert hanger hook. Tack design fabric to hanger.

2. To form leaves, cut blue-green ribbon into three 4" pieces. Fold ribbon with triangular points at center and press; slightly overlap ribbon bases and tack. Repeat for remaining two ribbon pieces. Set aside.

3. To form ribbon rose with variegated ribbon, fold one end to front twice, pinch wire near darker edge and carefully gather darker edge of ribbon along its wire. Roll gathered ribbon around folded end to form rose. Fold remaining end ⅛" to back twice to hide cut end. Tack rose at base to hold all gathers and folds in place.

4. Arrange the three leaves near base of hook and hot-glue to front of design fabric. Center and hot-glue rose over leaves.

5. Using white ribbon, tie bow around hook at the back of the hanger. Decoratively trim ribbon ends.

MATERIALS

Completed design
1¼ yards of ¼"-wide blue-green satin ribbon
1 yard of 1¾"-wide white double-edged gathered
   lace
¼ yard of white fabric and matching thread
Stuffing

DIRECTIONS

1. Cut one 6½" x 4¼" piece, one 6½" x 4½" piece, and two 7½" x 7½" pieces from the white fabric.

2. To make inner pillow form: with right sides facing, sew 7½" squares together, leaving a 3" opening along one side. Clip corners, turn right side out, and stuff. Slipstitch opening closed.

3. Hem one long edge of larger white fabric piece by turning edge under ¼" and then ½"; press and top-stitch. Repeat for smaller piece.

4. On larger piece, fold under ½" the remaining raw edges and press. Repeat for smaller piece.

5. With wrong sides facing, pin smaller piece to back of design fabric and with the stitched hem toward the center. Repeat with larger piece, overlapping the smaller piece. Topstitch.

6. Beginning at one corner, tack lace to pillow front at inside edge of Battenberg-lace trim.

7. Cut ribbon in half and tie two multi-looped bows (loops approximately ¾" lengths). Tack one bow at each lower corner at gathering seam of lace. Decoratively cut ribbon ends to a 6" length.

8. Insert pillow form.

Pansy-n-Ivy Pillow

Stitched on white Aida 14 over one thread, the finished design size is 3⅞" x 3¾". The fabric was cut 5¼" x 5¼" and trimmed with 2"-wide Battenberg lace. The design is taken from the Pansy-n-Ivy Circle graph on page 112.

FABRIC	DESIGN SIZES
Aida 11	4⅞" x 4¾"
Aida 18	3" x 2⅞"
Hardanger 22	2½" x 2⅜"

Stitch count: 54 x 52

Anchor   DMC (used for sample)

Step 1: Cross-stitch (2 strands)

1	⌐	White	
386	+	746	Off White
301	△	744	Yellow-pale
323	⅋	722	Orange Spice-lt.
303	◯	742	Tangerine-lt.
48	U	818	Baby Pink
85	+	3609	Plum-ultra lt.
86	∴	3608	Plum-vy. lt.
88	╱	718	Plum
108	◇	211	Lavender-lt.
101	●	550	Violet-vy. dk.
117	⅋	3747	Blue Violet-vy. lt.
118	■	340	Blue Violet-med.
158	□	3756	Baby Blue-ultra vy. lt.
159	•	827	Blue-vy. lt.

160	I	813	Blue-lt.
161	∴	826	Blue-med.
162	✕	825	Blue-dk.
265	I	3348	Yellow Green-lt.
266	◯	3347	Yellow Green-med.
268	▲	3345	Hunter Green-dk.
213	•	369	Pistachio Green-vy. lt.
214	△	368	Pistachio Green-lt.
216	✕	367	Pistachio Green-dk.
351	╱	400	Mahogany-dk.

Pansies–n–Ivy Circle **Stitch count: 54 x 52**

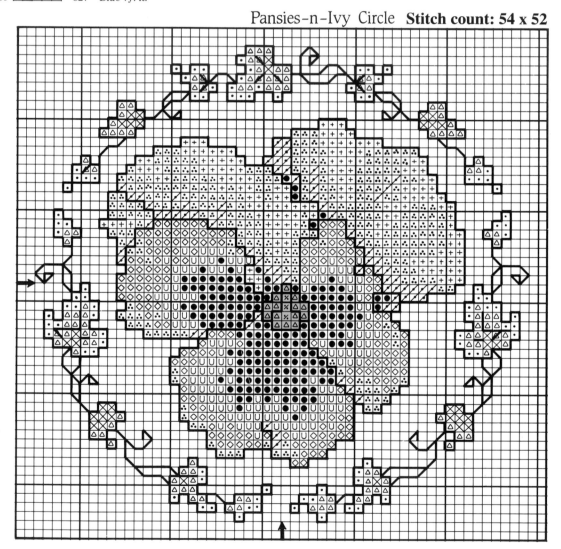

Step 2: Backstitch (1 strand)

101		550	Violet-vy. dk. (pink, purple, blue flowers, monograms)
162		825	Blue-dk. (flower pot)
216		367	Pistachio Green-dk. (ivy leaves)
268		3345	Hunter Green-dk. (pansy leaves)
351		400	Mahogany-dk. (yellow-orange pansies)

Step 3: Long Loose Stitches (1 strand)

351		400	Mahogany-dk.

Pansies-n-Ivy Corners **Stitch count: 48 x 48**

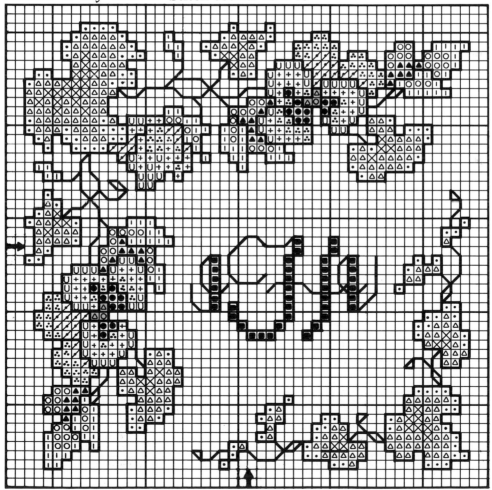

Ivy Alphabet

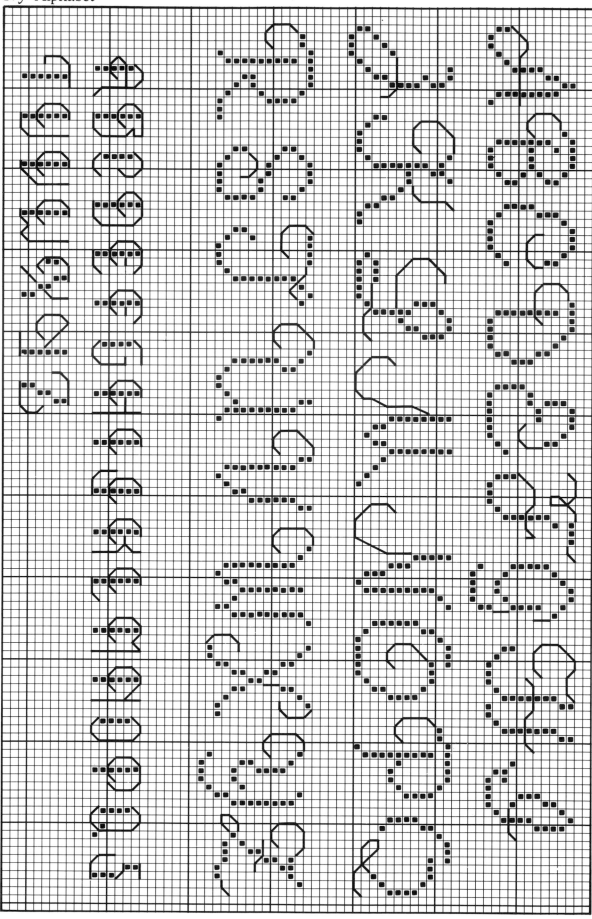

HANDFUL OF PANSIES NECKROLL

Stitched on white waste canvas 14 over one thread, the finished design size is 2¼" x 5½". The fabric was cut 5" x 9". The design is taken from the Vertical Pansy Border graph on page 120.

FABRIC   **DESIGN SIZES**
Aida 11   2⅞ x 6⅞"
Aida 18   1¾" x 4¼"
Hardanger 22   1⅜" x 3½"

Stitch count: 31 x 76

MATERIALS
5" x 9" piece of waste canvas 14
17"-long premade white Battenberg-lace neckroll
    pillow (size includes ruffles)
1¼ yards of ¼"-wide blue-green satin ribbon
1¼ yards of ¼"-wide lavender satin ribbon
1¼ yards of ⅞"-wide lavender satin ribbon
1¼ yards of ⅝"-wide white scalloped wedding
    lace trim
1¼ yards of 2"-wide white wedding lace trim
White sewing thread
Masking tape
Tweezers

DIRECTIONS
1. Remove inner pillow form from pillow. Clip back seam to open pillow top.

2. Tape edges of waste canvas. Center and baste waste canvas to pillow top.

3. Center and cross-stitch upper motif of Vertical Pansy Border design.

4. Slightly moisten waste canvas and with tweezers gently remove individual waste canvas threads.

5. With right sides facing, sew back seam. Turn right side out and insert pillow form.

6. Cut narrow lavender ribbon in half and replace original white ribbon ties at each end of pillow.

7. Cut blue-green ribbon in half. Beginning at back seam, pin and tack ribbons around pillow ⅜" from either side of design, overlapping ends and folding top ribbon end to back.

8. Cut scalloped lace trim in half. Pin trim over blue-green ribbon. Tack lace to pillow, enclosing the blue-green ribbon.

9. Cut wide lavender ribbon in half. Pin and tack around pillow ⅝" from each ruffle.

10. Cut wide lace trim in half and pin over wide ribbon. Tack lace to pillow, enclosing lavender ribbon.

PLEASANT PANSY CUSHION

Stitched on white waste canvas 14 over one thread, the finished design size is 7¼" x 3⅞". The fabric was cut 10" x 7". The design is taken from the Horizontal Pansy Border graph on page 120.

FABRIC	DESIGN SIZES
Aida 11	9⅛" x 5"
Aida 18	5⅝" x 3"
Hardanger 22	4⅝" x 2½"

Stitch count: 182 x 55

MATERIALS

16½"-square premade white Battenberg-lace pillow (size includes lace and ruffle trim)
10" x 7" piece of waste canvas
1⅜ yards of 1¼"-wide white double-edged lace with white ribbon through central beading
White sewing thread
Masking tape
Tweezers

DIRECTIONS

1. Remove inner pillow form from pillow. Clip seams and remove pillow back for easier stitching, if desired.

2. Tape edges of waste canvas. Center and baste waste canvas to pillow top.

3. Center and cross-stitch center portion of Horizontal Pansy Border (omit large ivy leaf and its accompanying smaller leaves and vines at each end of the design; see photo).

4. Moisten waste canvas slightly and with tweezers gently remove individual waste canvas threads.

5. Cut lace into four equal lengths. Mark with pins the middle of each side. Angle and baste lace strips across each corner of pillow front, beginning and ending each strip at pin placement. Topstitch in place.

6. Replace pillow back and insert pillow form.

PANSY FLAP ENVELOPE

Stitched ¼" from one corner on white Aida 14 over one thread, the finished design size is 3⅜" x 3⅜". The fabric was cut 9¼" x 9¼" and trimmed with 2 ¼"-wide Battenberg lace. The design is taken from the Pansy-n-Ivy Corner (pansies only) graph on page 113.

FABRIC	DESIGN SIZES
Aida 11	4⅜" x 4⅜"
Aida 18	2⅝" x 2⅝"
Hardanger 22	2⅛" x 2⅛"

Stitch count: 48 x 48

MATERIALS

Completed design
3 yards of ⅜"-wide pale yellow satin ribbon
19½"-square premade Battenberg-lace trimmed pillow

DIRECTIONS

1. Position design fabric over upper edge of pillow with design corner hanging down like an envelope flap. Tack through the lace areas of the design fabric and pillow.

2. Cut ribbon into three 11" lengths and thread each length into Battenberg lace at the sides and bottom of the pillow (see photo). Fold ends of ribbon under ⅛" and behind the lace and tack in place. Note: If necessary, adapt ribbon lengths to suit your particular pillow.

3. Cut remaining ribbon in half and thread each length from adjacent corners to the design corner. Fold end of ribbon under ⅛" and tack at adjacent corners. Tie bow at design corner.

Upright Pansy Plant **Stitch count: 54 x 81**

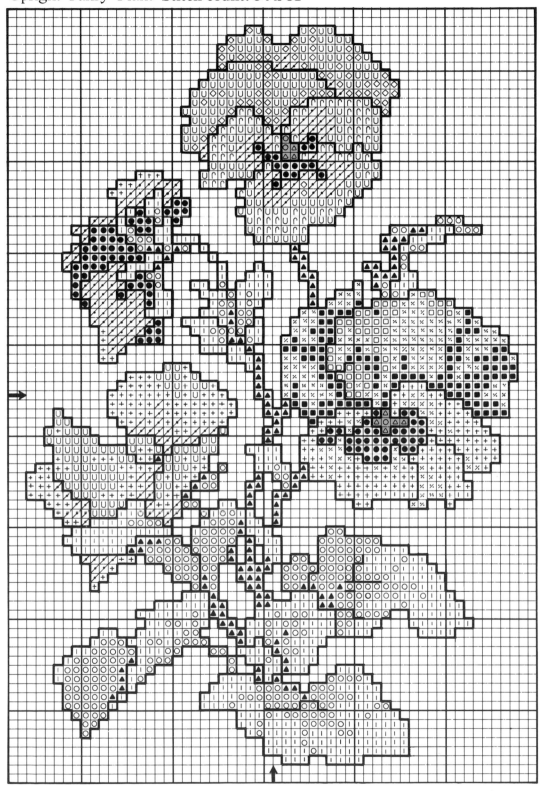

Vertical Pansy Border **Stitch count: 31 x 133**

Top

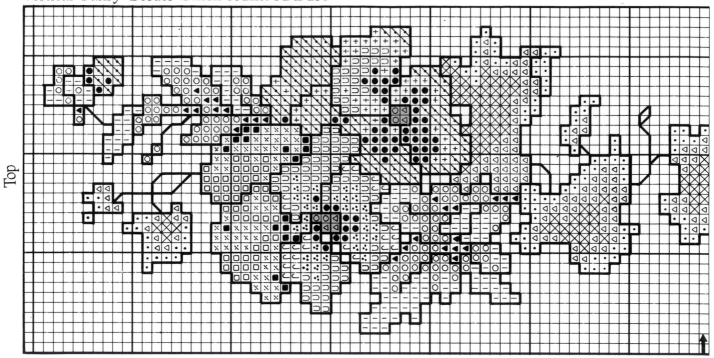

Horiontal Pansy Border **Stitch count: 182 x 55**

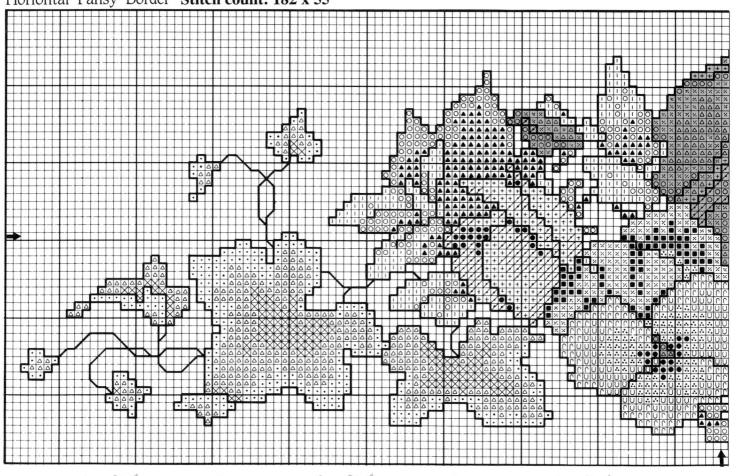

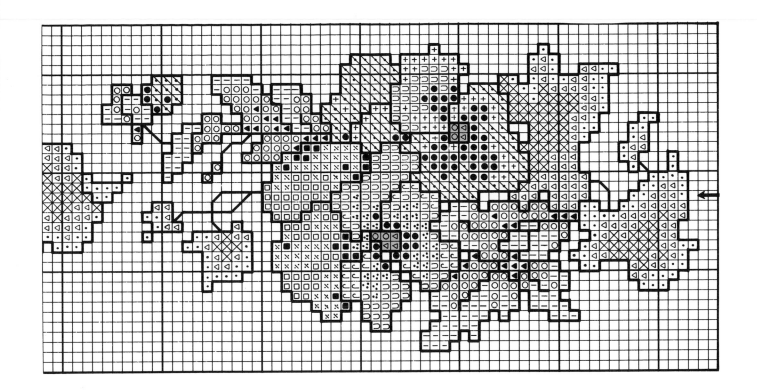

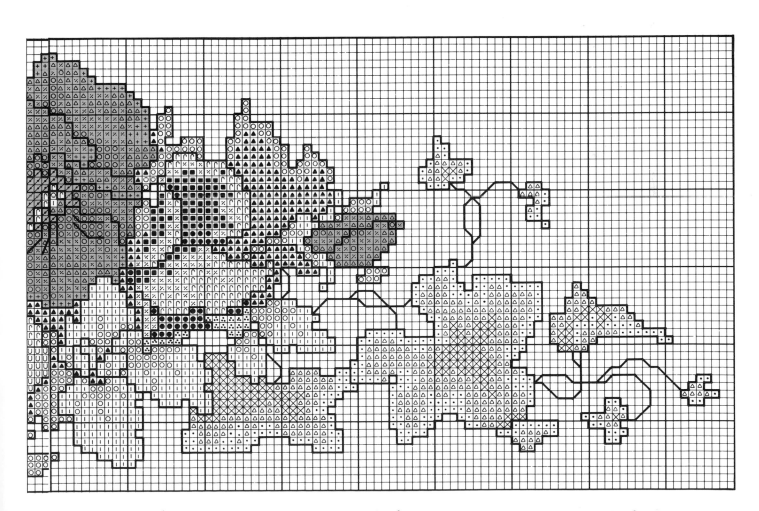

FAMILY ROOM

Where there is room in the heart, there is always room in the house.

Moore

SOLID FOOTING

Stitched on white mono canvas 12 over one thread, the finished design size is 13⅜" x 13⅜". The fabric was cut 18" x 18". Complete background in color 499. See photo on page 128.

FABRIC

FABRIC	DESIGN SIZES
Aida 11	14⅝" x 14⅝"
Aida 14	11½" x 11½"
Aida 18	9" x 9"
Hardanger 22	7⅜" x 7⅜"

MATERIALS

Completed design
Queen Anne footstool (12" x 12" x 8")
Staple gun and ¼" staples

DIRECTIONS

1. Block design if necessary.

2. Unscrew and remove cushion top from footstool.

3. Center design fabric (right side up) over cushion. Pull canvas edges to back of cushion and staple.

4. Reattach cushion to footstool.

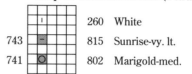

DMC Floss		Paternayan Persian Yarn (used for sample)	
	Step 1:	Continental-stitch (2 strands)	
	ı	260	White
743	–	815	Sunrise-vy. lt.
741	O	802	Marigold-med.

Solid Footing (Top Left) **Stitch count: 161 x 161**

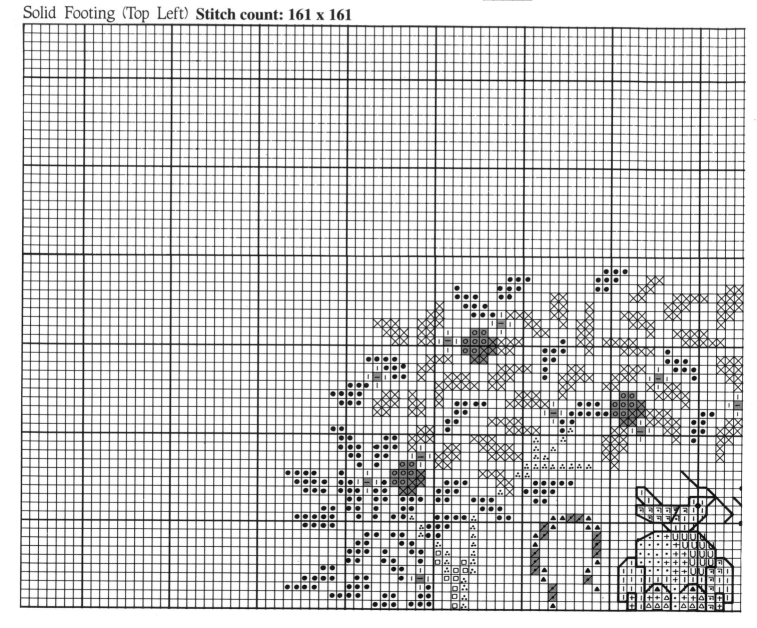

922	☒	883	Ginger-med.	839	∴	461	Beige Brown-dk.
3778	△	863	Copper	762	▣	204	Steel Gray-vy. lt.
356	⁖	861	Copper-vy. dk.	310	▲	220	Black
472	⁄	694	Loden Green-lt.
3013	⊠	653	Olive Green-med.

Step 2: Backstitch (2 strands DMC floss)

524	○	605	Forest Green-vy. lt.
522	●	603	Forest Green-med.
964	+	594	Caribbean Blue-lt.
519	⊡	584	Sky Blue-lt.
334	△	503	Federal Blue-med.
553	⟋	312	Grape-med.
552	▢	311	Grape-dk.
739		499	Wicker Brown-vy. lt. (background)
738	·	498	Wicker Brown-lt.
437	+	497	Wicker Brown-med.
436	U	496	Wicker Brown-dk.
434	■	412	Earth Brown-med.
841	▢	463	Beige Brown-lt.

522	603	Forest Green-med. (1 strand Paternayan Persian Yarn: olive branch)
550	550	Violet-vy. dk. (inside dress)
434	434	Brown-lt. (faces, hands)
801	801	Coffee Brown-dk. (rabbits, vines)
3022	3022	Brown Gray-med. (hair, birds, necklace)
310	310	Black (all else)

Step 3: French Knot (2 strands DMC floss)

3022	◆	3022	Brown Gray-med.
310	●	310	Black

Solid Footing (Top Right)

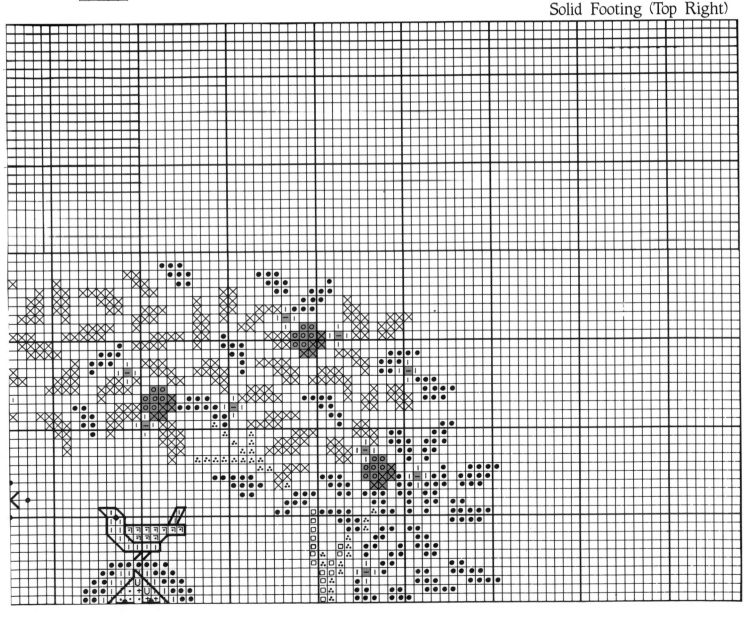

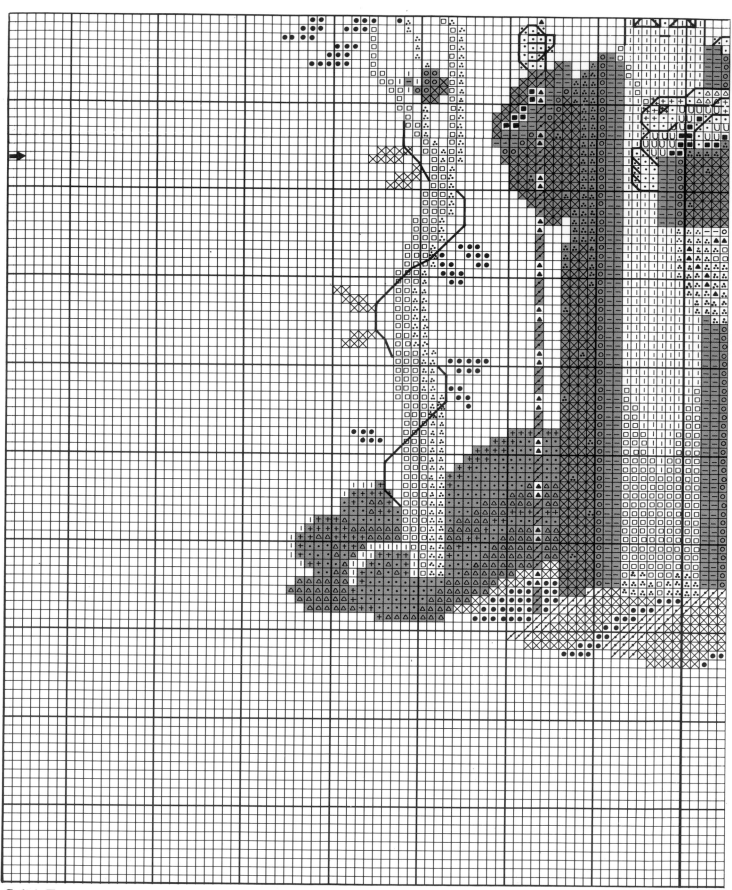

Solid Footing (Bottom Left)

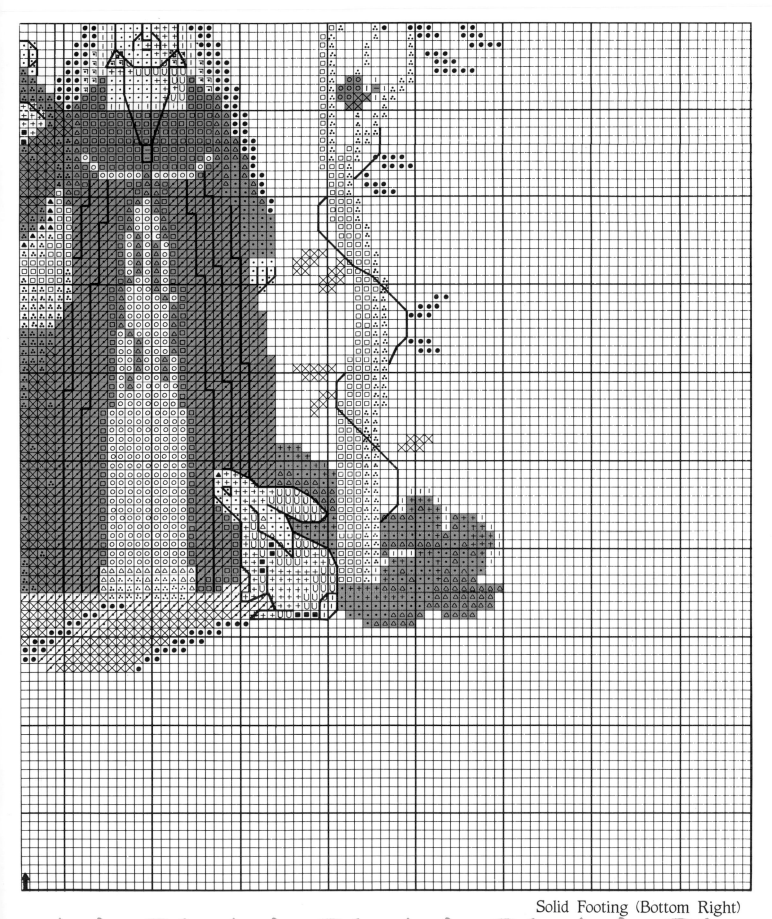

Solid Footing (Bottom Right)

FAMILIES AFGHAN

Stitched on ivory Anne afghan cloth 18 over two threads, the finished design size is 29¾" x 23½". The fabric was cut 45" x 58". The graph shows only the bottom half of the border and vine box. Invert pages showing the border, connect to the bottom half, and continue border and vine design to complete the box.

FABRIC	DESIGN SIZES
Aida 11	24⅜" x 19¼"
Aida 14	19⅛" x 15⅛"
Aida 18	14⅞" x 11¾"
Hardanger 22	12⅛" x 9⅝"

MATERIALS
Afghan with completed design
Ivory sewing thread

DIRECTIONS
1. Pull out 45th thread beyond brown border on all sides. Sew narrow zigzag over next two threads towards design.

2. Trim design fabric to 5½" beyond zigzag line on all sides. Fringe.

TWO BY TWO PILLOW

Stitched on beige Aida 11 over one thread, the finished design size is 4⅜" x 3½". The fabric was cut 14" x 13". The Foxes design is taken from the Families Afghan graph on page 131.

FABRIC	DESIGN SIZES
Aida 14	3⅜" x 2¾"
Aida 18	2⅝" x 2⅛"
Hardanger 22	2⅛" x 1¾"

Stitch count: 48 x 38

MATERIALS
Completed design
⅜ yard of gold damask fabric
⅜ yard of beige fabric and matching thread
Stuffing

DIRECTIONS
All seam allowances are ½".

1. Using two strands each of DMC 402 and 976, cross-stitch over the 14th rows surrounding the design.

2. Trim design fabric to 9" x 10" with the design centered.

3. Cut two 11" x 12" pieces of damask fabric for pillow back; cut two 9" x 10" pieces of beige fabric.

4. Baste design fabric to one beige piece.

5. With right sides facing, sew design fabric piece and remaining beige piece together, leaving a 5" opening along the bottom. Clip corners and turn right side out. Slipstitch opening closed and press.

6. With right sides facing, sew gold pieces together, leaving a 5" opening along one side. Clip corners and turn right side out. Slipstitch opening closed and press.

7. Center design piece over pillow back and baste in place.

8. Topstitch 1" from edge of design piece and adjacent to cross-stitch rows, leaving a 5" opening in the bottom seam.

9. Stuff inner area (be sure that corners are stuffed).

10. Topstitch opening closed.

307	⁒	⁄	977	Golden Brown-lt.
347	I	⁄	402	Mahogany-vy. lt. (2 strands)
308			976	Golden Brown-med. (2 strands)
338	□	◱	3776	Mahogany-lt.
324	◇	◿	921	Copper
349	⋰	⁄	301	Mahogany-med.
351	▲	◿	400	Mahogany-dk.
370	⋰	◿	434	Brown-lt.
379	–	◿	840	Beige Brown-med.
380	◿	⁄	839	Beige Brown-dk.
357	▢	◿	801	Coffee Brown-dk.
900	·	◿	3024	Brown Gray-vy. lt.
8581	△	◿	647	Beaver Gray-med.
905	⊠	◿	646	Beaver Gray-dk.
398	+	⁄	415	Pearl Gray
400	△	◿	317	Pewter Gray
403	●	◔	310	Black

Step 2: Backstitch (2 strands)

147		312	Navy Blue-lt. (water)
215		320	Pistachio Green-med. (leaves, palm trees)
878		501	Blue Green-dk. (ivy stems, white flowers, grass)
338		3776	Mahogany-lt. (in yellow of ark, plank)
351		400	Mahogany-dk. (roof of ark, border, giraffes, brown on foxes)
380		839	Beige Brown-dk. (ark except windows, trees, water buffalos except manes, olive branch)
905		646	Beaver Gray-dk. (birds, sheep, white on foxes)
401		844	Beaver Gray-ultra dk. (elephants)
403		310	Black (all else)

Anchor   DMC (used for sample)

Step 1: Cross-stitch (4 strands)

1	·	⁄		White
891	U	⁄	676	Old Gold-lt.
928	+	◿	598	Turquoise-lt.
168	○	◔	807	Peacock Blue
161	▣	⁄	3760	Wedgewood-med.
147	U	◿	312	Navy Blue-lt.
265	⁄	⁄	3348	Yellow Green-lt.
843	○	◔	3364	Pine Green
215	⊠	◿	320	Pistachio Green-med.
878	■	◱	501	Blue Green-dk.
942	▣	⁄	738	Tan-vy. lt.

Step 3: French Knot (2 strands)

905	◆	646	Beaver Gray-dk.
403	■	310	Black
307	●	977	Golden Brown-lt. (8 strands)

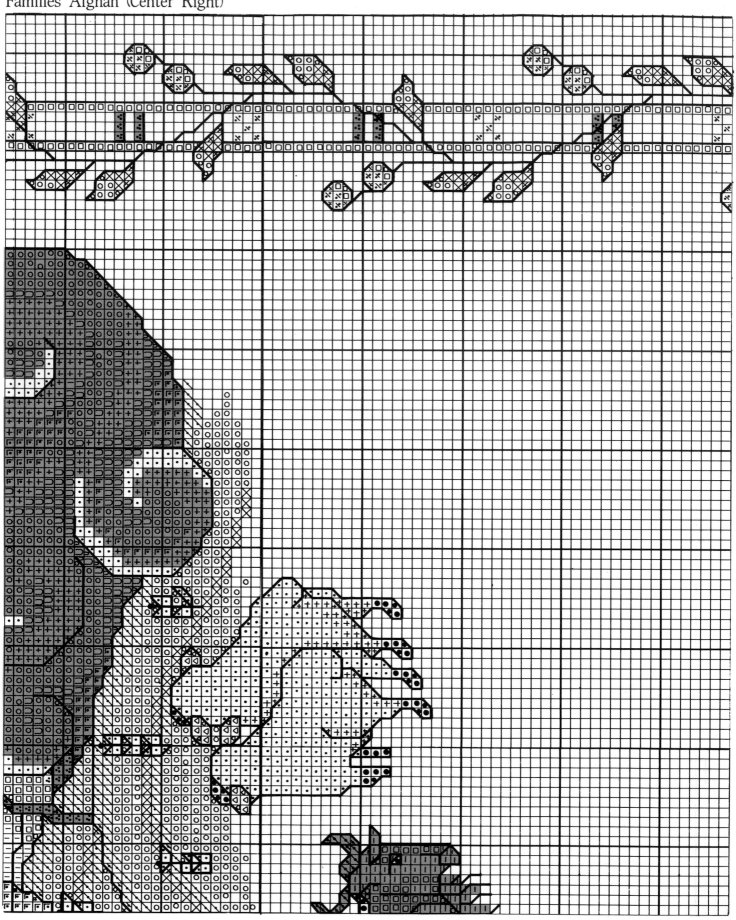

Families Afghan (Bottom Right)

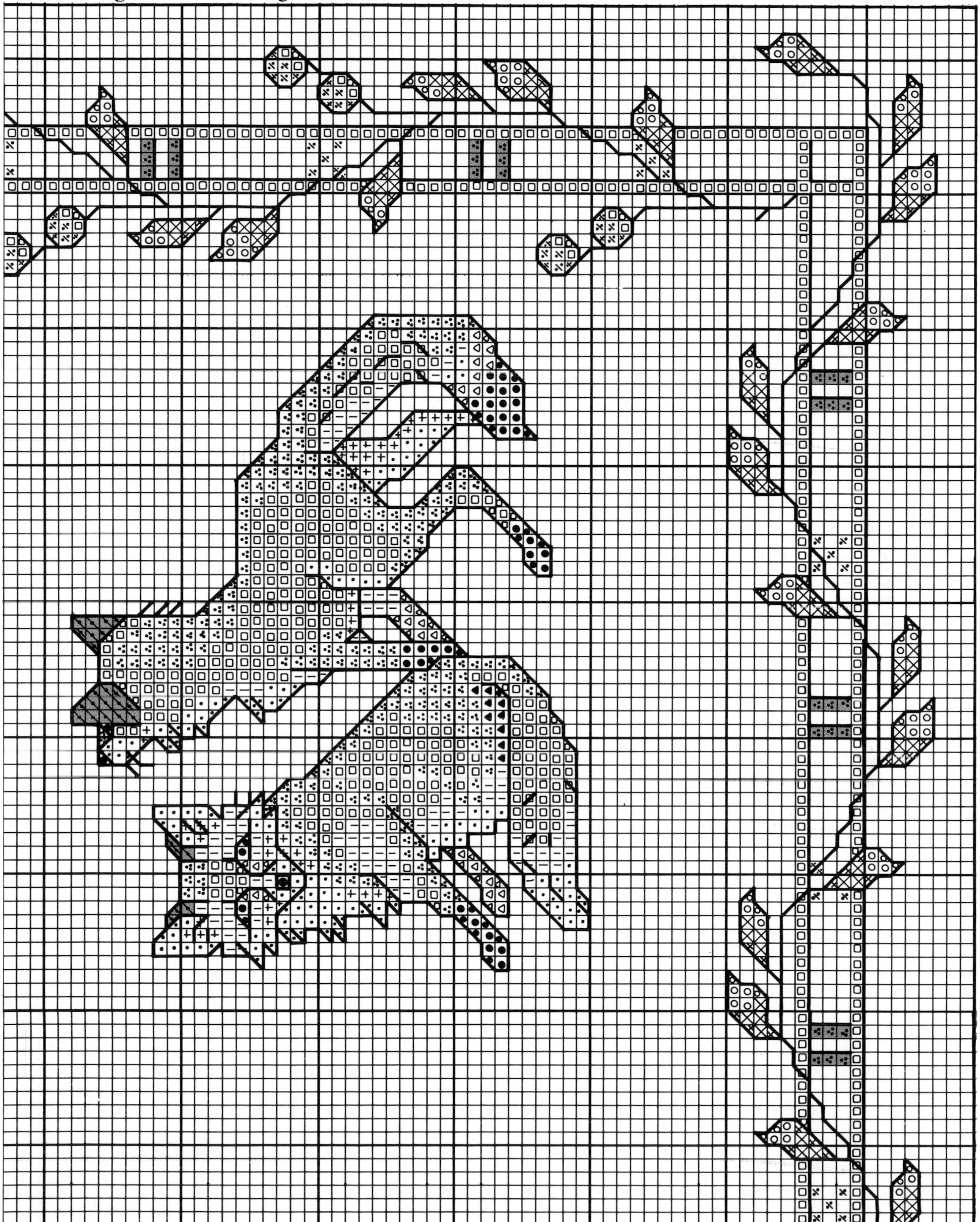

Top

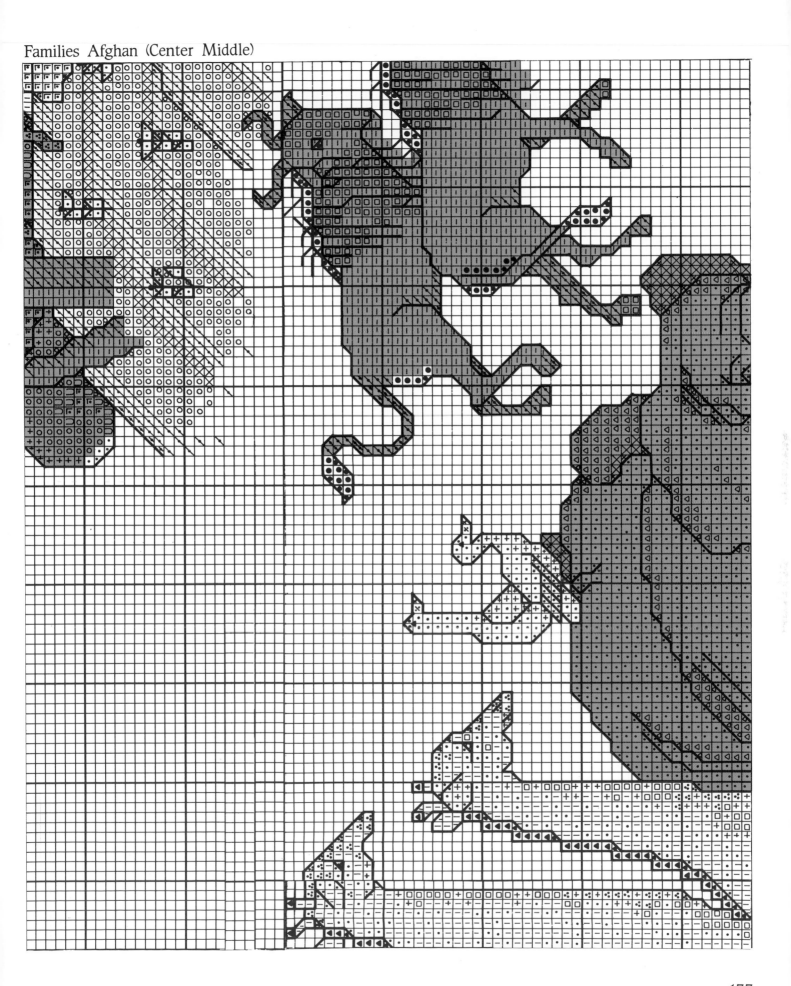

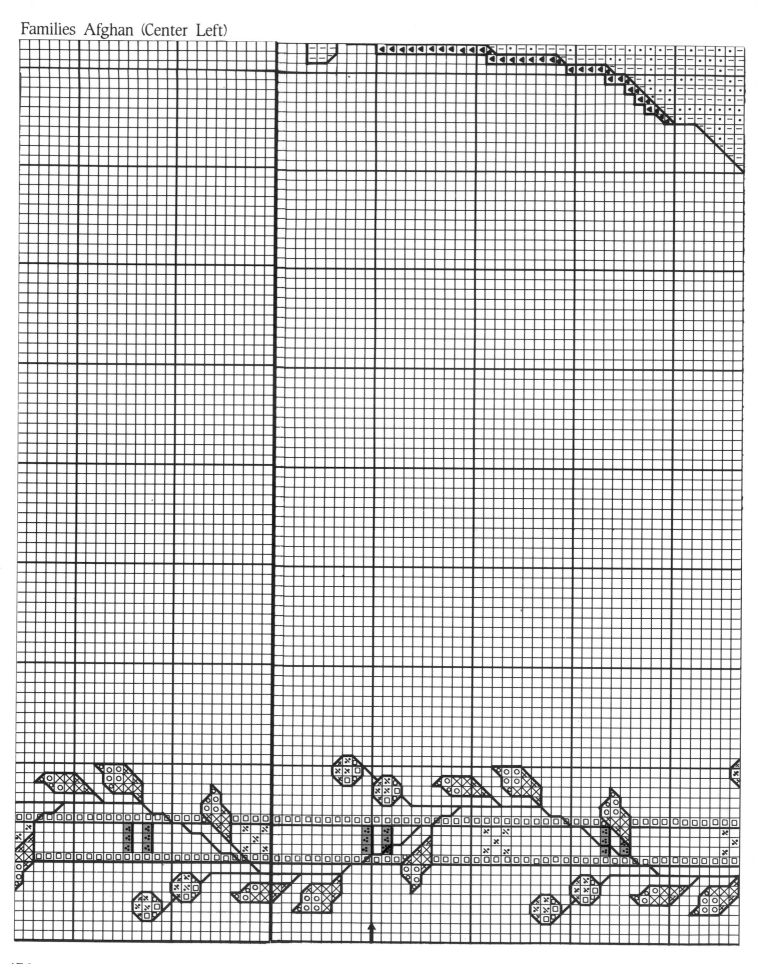

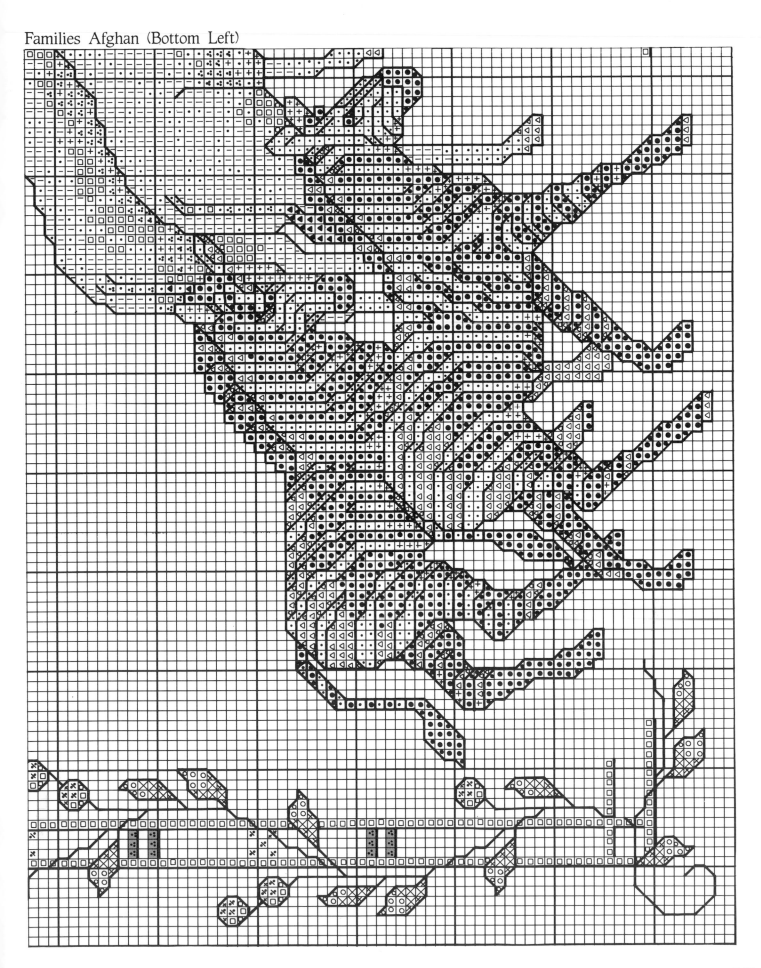

GENERAL INSTRUCTIONS

CROSS-STITCH

Fabrics: Counted cross-stitch is usually worked on even-weave fabric. These fabrics are manufactured specifically for counted, thread embroidery and are woven with the same number of vertical as horizontal threads per inch. Because the number of threads in the fabric is equal in each direction, each stitch will be the same size. It is the number of threads per inch in even-weave fabrics that determines the size of a finished design.

Waste Canvas: Waste canvas is a coarse, fabric-like substance used as a guide for cross-stitching on fabrics other than even-weaves. Cut the waste canvas 1" larger on all sides than the finished design size. Baste it to the fabric to be stitched. Complete the stitching. Then, dampen the stitched area with cold water. Pull the waste canvas threads out one at a time with tweezers. It is easier to pull all the threads running in one direction first; then pull out the opposite threads. Allow the stitching to dry. Place face down on a towel and iron.

Preparing Fabric: Cut even-weave fabric at least 3" larger on all sides than the design size, or cut it the size specified in the instructions. If the item is to be finished into a pillow, for example, the fabric should be cut as directed. A 3" margin is the minimum amount of space that allows for comfortably working the edges of the design. To prevent fraying, whipstitch or machine-zigzag raw fabric edges.

Needles: Needles should slip easily through the holes in the fabric but not pierce the fabric. Use a blunt tapestry needle, size 24 or 26. Never leave the needle in the design area of your work. It can leave rust or a permanent impression on the fabric.

Floss: All numbers and color names are cross-referenced between Paternayan Persian Yarn and Anchor and DMC brands of floss. Run the floss over a damp sponge to straighten. Separate all six strands and use the number of strands called for in the code.

Centering the Design: Fold the fabric in half horizontally, then vertically. Place a pin in the fold point to mark the center. Locate the center of the design on the graph by following the vertical and horizontal arrows in the left and bottom margins. Begin stitching all designs at the center point of the graph and the fabric unless the instructions indicate otherwise.

Graphs: Each symbol represents a different color. Make one stitch for each symbol, referring to the code to verify which stitch to use. Use the small arrows in the margins to find the center of the graph. When a graph is continued, the sections are titled according to top, bottom, left, middle and right, indicating where to connect them. The stitch count is printed with each graph, listing first the width, then the length, of the design.

Codes: The code indicates the brand of thread used to stitch the model, as well as the cross-reference for using another brand. The steps in the code identify the stitch to be used and the number of floss strands for that stitch. The symbols match the graph, and give the color number and name for the thread. A symbol under a diagonal line indicates a half cross-stitch. Blended threads are represented on the code and graph with a single symbol, but both color names are listed.

Securing the Floss: Insert your needle up from the underside of the fabric at your starting point. Hold 1" of thread behind the fabric and stitch over it, securing with the first few stitches. To finish thread, run under four or more stitches on the back of the design. Never knot floss unless working on clothing. Another method of securing floss is the waste knot. Knot your floss and insert your needle from the right side of the fabric about 1" from the design area. Work several stitches over the thread to secure. Cut off the knot later.

Stitching: For a smooth cross-stitch, use the "push-and-pull" method. Push the needle straight down and completely through fabric before pulling. Do not pull the thread tightly. Consistent tension throughout ensures even stitches. Make one stitch for every symbol on the chart. To stitch in rows, work from left to right and then back. Half-crosses are used to make a rounded shape. Make the longer stitch in the direction of the slanted line.

Carrying Floss:
To carry floss, weave floss under the previously worked stitches on the back. Do not carry thread across any fabric that is not or will not be stitched. Loose threads, especially dark ones, will show through the fabric.

Twisted Floss:
If floss is twisted, drop the needle and allow the floss to unwind itself. Floss will cover best when lying flat. Use thread no longer than 18" because it will tend to twist and knot.

Cleaning Completed Work:
When stitching is complete, soak it in cold water with a mild soap for five to ten minutes. Rinse well and roll in a towel to remove excess water. Do not wring. Place work face down on a dry towel and iron on a warm setting until dry.

Cross-stitch:
Make one cross for each symbol on the chart. Bring needle and thread up at A, down at B, up at C, and down again at D. For rows, stitch from left to right, then back. All stitches should lie in the same direction.

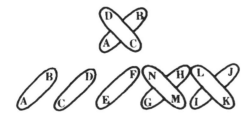

Half Cross-stitch:
The stitch actually fits three-fourths of the area. Make the longer stitch in the direction of the slanted line on the graph. Bring needle and thread up at A, down at B, up at C, and down at D.

Backstitch:
Complete all cross-stitching before working backstitches or other accent stitches. Working from left to right with one strand of floss (unless designated otherwise on code), bring needle and thread up at A, down at B, and up again at C. Go back down at A and continue in this manner.

French Knot:
Bring needle up at A, using one strand of embroidery floss. Wrap floss around needle two times (unless indicated otherwise in instructions). Insert needle beside A, pulling floss until it fits snugly around needle. Pull needle through to back.

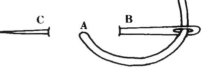

Special Stitches:

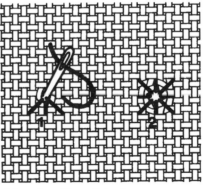

Algerian Eye Stitch

Florentine Stitch

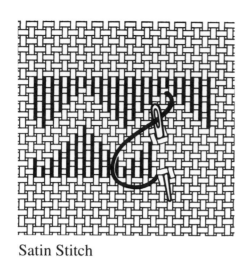

Satin Stitch

Long Loose Stitch:
Secure thread by running ends through existing cross-stitch on back. Enter at point from wrong side of fabric and exit at end point.

SEWING HINTS

Patterns:
Use tracing paper to trace patterns. Be sure to transfer all information. All patterns include seam allowances. The seam allowance is ½" unless otherwise specified.

Marking on Fabric:
Always use a dressmaker's pen or chalk to mark on fabric. It will wash out when you clean your finished piece.

Slipstitch:
Insert needle at A, taking a small stitch, and slide it through the folded edge of the fabric about ⅛" to ¼", bringing it out at B.

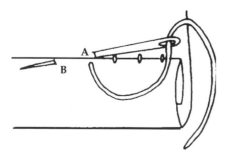

Enlarging a Pattern:
All patterns are a reduction of the original size unless specified otherwise. Enlarge patterns to the indicated percentage using a photocopy machine. It is best to use a professional copy center.

Bias Strips:
Bias strips are used for ruffles, binding or corded piping. To cut bias, fold the fabric at a 45-degree angle to the grain of the fabric and crease. Cut on the crease. Cut additional strips the width indicated in the instructions and parallel to the first cutting line. The ends of the bias strips should be on the grain of the fabric. Place the right sides of the ends together and stitch with a ½" seam. Continue to piece the strips until they are the length that is indicated in the instructions.

Corded Piping:
Center cording on the wrong side of the bias strip and fold the fabric over it, aligning raw edges. Using a zipper foot, stitch through both layers of fabric close to the cording. Trim the seam allowance to ¼".

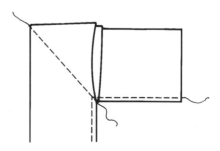

Mitering a Corner:
Sew border strips up to, but not through, the seam allowance; backstitch. Repeat on all four edges, making stitching lines meet exactly at the corners. Fold two adjacent border pieces together. Mark; then stitch at a 45-degree angle. Trim seam allowance to ¼".

Blocking:
Stretch and shape piece right side up and pin in place on covered piece of cardboard . Spray with cold water from a fine-mist spray bottle until damp. Allow to dry away from direct sunlight or heat. A warm atmosphere is best for drying.

METRIC EQUIVALENCY CHART

MM-Millimetres   CM-Centimetres

INCHES TO MILLIMETRES AND CENTIMETRES

INCHES	MM	CM	INCHES	CM	INCHES	CM
⅛	3	0.3	9	22.9	30	76.2
¼	6	0.6	10	25.4	31	78.7
½	13	1.3	12	30.5	33	83.8
⅝	16	1.6	13	33.0	34	86.4
¾	19	1.9	14	35.6	35	88.9
⅞	22	2.2	15	38.1	36	91.4
1	25	2.5	16	40.6	37	94.0
1¼	32	3.2	17	43.2	38	96.5
1½	38	3.8	18	45.7	39	99.1
1¾	44	4.4	19	48.3	40	101.6
2	51	5.1	20	50.8	41	104.1
2½	64	6.4	21	53.3	42	106.7
3	76	7.6	22	55.9	43	109.2
3½	89	8.9	23	58.4	44	111.8
4	102	10.2	24	61.0	45	114.3
4½	114	11.4	25	63.5	46	116.8
5	127	12.7	26	66.0	47	119.4
6	152	15.2	27	68.6	48	121.9
7	178	17.8	28	71.1	49	124.5
8	203	20.3	29	73.7	50	127.0

YARDS TO METRES

YARDS	METRES	YARDS	METRES	YARDS	METRES	YARDS	METRES	YARDS	METRES
⅛	0.11	2⅛	1.94	4⅛	3.77	6⅛	5.60	8⅛	7.43
¼	0.23	2¼	2.06	4¼	3.89	6¼	5.72	8¼	7.54
⅜	0.34	2⅜	2.17	4⅜	4.00	6⅜	5.83	8⅜	7.66
½	0.46	2½	2.29	4½	4.11	6½	5.94	8½	7.77
⅝	0.57	2⅝	2.40	4⅝	4.23	6⅝	6.06	8⅝	7.89
¾	0.69	2¾	2.51	4¾	4.34	6¾	6.17	8¾	8.00
⅞	0.80	2⅞	2.63	4⅞	4.46	6⅞	6.29	8⅞	8.12
1	0.91	3	2.74	5	4.57	7	6.40	9	8.23
1⅛	1.03	3⅛	2.86	5⅛	4.69	7⅛	6.52	9⅛	8.34
1¼	1.14	3¼	2.97	5¼	4.80	7¼	6.63	9¼	8.46
1⅜	1.26	3⅜	3.09	5⅜	4.91	7⅜	6.74	9⅜	8.57
1½	1.37	3½	3.20	5½	5.03	7½	6.86	9½	8.69
1⅝	1.49	3⅝	3.31	5⅝	5.14	7⅝	6.97	9⅝	8.80
1¾	1.60	3¾	3.43	5¾	5.26	7¾	7.09	9¾	8.92
1⅞	1.71	3⅞	3.54	5⅞	5.37	7⅞	7.20	9⅞	9.03
2	1.83	4	3.66	6	5.49	8	7.32	10	9.14

INDEX

What is a home? A roof to keep out the rain. Four walls to keep out the wind. Floors to keep out the cold. Yes, but a home is more than that. It is the laugh of a baby, the song of a mother, the strength of a father. Warmth of loving hearts, light from happy eyes, kindness, loyalty, and comradeship. This is a home.
May God bless it.

Ernestine Shuman-Heink

144